Investing for Income

A Guide to Earning
Top Interest on Your Savings

HUGH ANDERSON

THE GLOBE AND MAIL

D1396570

Penguin Books

PENGUIN BOOKS
Published by the Penguin Group
Penguin Books Canada Ltd., 2801 John Street, Markham, Ontario L3R 1B4
Penguin Books Ltd., 27 Wrights Lane, London W8 5TZ, England
Viking Penguin Inc., 40 West 23rd Street, New York, New York 10010, USA
Penguin Books Australia Ltd., Ringwood, Victoria, Australia
Penguin Books (NZ) Ltd., 182-190 Wairau Road, Auckland 10, New Zealand
Penguin Books Ltd., Registered Offices: Harmondsworth, Middlesex, England

Published in Penguin Books, 1996

10 9 8 7 6 5 4 3 2 1
Copyright © The Globe and Mail, 1996
All inquiries should be addressed to Globe Information Services at 444 Front Street West,
Toronto, Ontario M5V 2S9 (416) 585-5250

Canadian Cataloguing in Publication Data
The National Library of Canada has catalogued this publication as follows:
Anderson, Hugh, 1935-
Investing for income (Toronto, Ont. : 1997)
  Investing for income : a guide to earning top interest on your savings

(The Globe and Mail personal finance library)
Annual.
1997-
Continues: Money for rent.

ISSN 1207-6392
ISBN 0-14-026254-7 (1996)

1. Fixed-income securities – Canada – Periodicals.
I. Title. II. Title: Series.

HG4527.T68   332.63'2044   C96-900750-7

Cover design: Creative Network
Cover illustration: Peter Yundt

CONTENTS

Tables and Illustrations

TABLES

CHARTS

Dedication

To Ena, once more, with love and admiration, for her research skills and for her tolerance of an often preoccupied and crotchety husband during the time it took to write the sixth edition of this second book.

Acknowledgements

My grateful thanks to:

David Abrams, my cousin the notary, who helped me understand the difficult business of becoming a mortgage lender.

Michel Duchesne, a proficient practitioner of bond market trading and investing, who was always willing to explain to an inquisitive journalist how his business works, but revealed no secrets.

Johanne Duc, my assistant, who found some needed information for me and dealt ably with clients' calls in my absence while I worked on this new edition.

Mark Lazarus, my brother-in-law the stockbroker, who enlightened me on the practical details of fixed-income investments as seen from the trenches.

Claire Stevens, an able accountant, who keeps me up to date on constantly changing tax rates and rules that affect investors.

Introduction

THIS BOOK IS FOR EVERYONE who has a bit of money to spare after paying the expenses of daily living, and for those strong-willed or fortunate souls who have a lot put aside already. It is also for those who plan, or hope, to be in either of those categories in the future. Charles Dickens' wonderful character Mr. Micawber once noted astutely that spending more than you get leads to misery and spending less than you get leads to happiness. That still leaves unanswered the question of what you do with the leftover cash when you achieve Mr. Micawber's definition of happiness.

You could, of course, keep the unspent cash under the mattress and perhaps take it out and count it every night. That would be free of charge, but would make your savings rather vulnerable to fires and burglars. You could dig a hole for it in the garden, but you might forget where you put it. What's more, a covetous neighbour might be watching. You could park it in a safety deposit box and count it during business hours. That would be more secure but it would cost you the annual fee for the box – probably tax-deductible, mind you.

Assume, anyway, that your money survived those risks. Hoarding it would still cost you a bundle. Money that sits around doing nothing loses its value with dismaying speed. At an inflation rate of about 5 per cent, a dollar's purchasing power shrinks to just 61 cents in a mere 10 years.

So what can you do, other than spend it quickly? You can use your money to make more money, and then use your profits to make still more money. From this insight many great fortunes have grown, by using money in highly rewarding ways to build a mighty financial mountain. True, such achievements are not for most of us. They require a special concentration on money-making that is a minority sport. There are too many other interesting things to do with your life than to spend all of it thinking about making money.

What you can do without too much trouble is lend or rent your money out to somebody else for a while, if only by putting it into a savings account at a bank, trust company or credit union. The rent you get when you do this is called interest. Eventually, you expect to get all your original cash back. You have merely lent it to somebody else to use in return for regular payments of interest, which in turn you can spend or relend as you wish.

This is the essence of fixed-income investing, in all its simple and complicated forms. Note carefully the word "lent," however. In most normal circumstances, a lender expects to be repaid every last dollar and cent that was lent, plus interest. So do fixed-income investors. They are not financial adventurers, ready to take risks of big losses for the prospect of making rewardingly large capital gains. Most large losses suffered by fixed-income investors result from forgetting that distinction.

The process works this way: Unlike a stock market investor, a fixed-income investor is prepared to accept a rate of return on money that is known at the start of the deal and usually does not vary. In addition, that rate of return will on average be lower than the long-term average return from investing in stocks. Over nearly 70 years from 1926 through 1995 the total return, including dividends and capital gains, on a representative selection of Canadian stocks averaged about 10 per cent a year. The annual average return on interest-paying fixed-income investments was roughly half that rate. No one should be surprised at this. If, on average and over time, stock market investors did not get a better return than fixed-income investors, they would stop buying stocks. So far, this has not happened, which is a good thing for an economy that thrives on profitable risk-taking.

The quid pro quo for accepting this lower average return is the expectation that a fixed-income investment will be less risky than a stock-market investment. This does not always turn out to be true but it is accurate often enough to be a good working assumption. Reading this book will help you make sure this assumption always applies to you.

In the early chapters, you will learn of the awesome power of compound interest and how to calculate it, of the huge size of the money-for-rent market and how to find out what's going on in it.

You will be guided through the first steps of accumulating some money to rent out and choosing from the bewildering array of savings accounts available. Government deposit insurance is explained along with the ins and outs of Canada Savings Bonds, an almost perfect investment for beginners, but usually available only once a year. Some advice on term deposits and guaranteed investment certificates precedes the intermediate course in interest calculations.

Then follows a wealth of information on investing in bonds, treasury bills, preferred shares and mortgages. The pros and cons of using mutual funds and leverage are discussed. The taxman's rules for fixed-income investment and keeping track of how you are doing follow. You learn how to plan a portfolio and the golden rule of fixed-income investments: Earn interest free of tax for as long as possible. Finally, the prospects for fixed-income investments in the 1990s are examined.

This is not a get-rich-quick book. Guides of that sort are best left on the shelf unread. They may make their authors rich but rarely their readers. It is perfectly possible to get rich quick from buying a winning lottery ticket or from marrying into money, but it is not probable. You might get rich fairly fast in the stock market, but it is more likely you will get into trouble if you try to accumulate a fortune too quickly.

Success for the fixed-income investor is the triumph of the tortoise over the hare. Start as soon as you can. Rent your money out for the best available fee, get it all back, rent it out again and do not take unnecessary risks. That is the way it is done. As the Roman emperor Augustus put it, with admirable economy of words: "Festina lente." More haste, less speed.

Good renting!

CHAPTER 1

The Power of Compound Interest

IF YOU HAD BEEN WEALTHY enough to buy a representative selection of Government of Canada marketable bonds at the beginning of 1982 and had sold them at the end of the year, you would have made an unusually large 35 per cent total return on your investment in just 12 months, including price changes and interest. That's your original stake, plus 35 cents of profit for each dollar invested.

Such a one-year gain is not to be sneezed at, especially when compared with the 5.5 per cent average total return that same year on the 300 stocks that make up the Toronto Stock Exchange composite index. It is, however, a long way from buying a stock and watching it double in six months. True, that sort of double-your-money thrill doesn't happen all that often, even in the stock market. Too frequently, in fact, the dominant emotion of stock market investors is the sick feeling you get from buying a stock and watching it go down instead of up. Nevertheless, the stock market's glamour is largely based on the possibility of super-large profits in super-quick time.

Why bother, then, to learn the ins and outs of fixed-income investing? It's because the remarkable power of compound interest can do wonders for your financial health, and in surprisingly short periods of time. However, you do have to be patient in the very early going, like a long-distance runner. Take a good look at the table and accompanying chart on the next two pages. They show how each dollar of your savings multiplies when earning 5 per cent simple interest a year for 30 years, compared with what happens when you get 5 per cent compound interest a year. The simple-interest calculations show the results if you take the five cents of interest received each year and stash it someplace where it gathers dust but not interest. The compound-interest calculations show what happens if you add each year's interest to the original amount and rent

The Power of Compound Interest

ANNUAL 5% RATE

Year	Compound amount	Simple amount
0	$1.00	$1.00
1	1.05	1.05
2	1.10	1.10
3	1.16	1.15
4	1.22	1.20
5	1.28	1.25
6	1.34	1.30
7	1.41	1.35
8	1.48	1.40
9	1.55	1.45
10	1.63	1.50
11	1.71	1.55
12	1.80	1.60
13	1.89	1.65
14	1.98	1.70
15	2.08	1.75
16	2.18	1.80
17	2.29	1.85
18	2.41	1.90
19	2.53	1.95
20	2.65	2.00
21	2.79	2.05
22	2.93	2.10
23	3.07	2.15
24	3.23	2.20
25	3.39	2.25
26	3.56	2.30
27	3.73	2.35
28	3.92	2.40
29	4.12	2.45
30	4.32	2.50

TABLE I

the whole pile out again at 5 per cent. There is an interesting difference between the results: $4.32 at the end of 30 years from compound interest, which is getting on to twice the amount at the end of 30 years from earning simple interest. It works this way: With simple interest, each year another five cents is added to the accumulated amount but nothing else is done. At the end of the first year you have $1.05, at the end of the second year $1.10, at the end of the third year $1.15 and so on. Over 30 years that adds up to a total of $1.50 in interest, which added to the original dollar increases your savings to $2.50. Nice, but not the way to get wealthy.

With compound interest, you also get five cents of interest at the end of the first year, but you take that profit and add it to your original dollar. Then you reinvest all of it. This means that in the second year you receive interest not just on your original dollar but on $1.05. In other words, you start to earn interest on the interest, which is the magic formula for success in fixed-income investing. At the end of the third year, therefore, you receive six cents instead of five cents. Your original dollar has turned into $1.16, not $1.15.

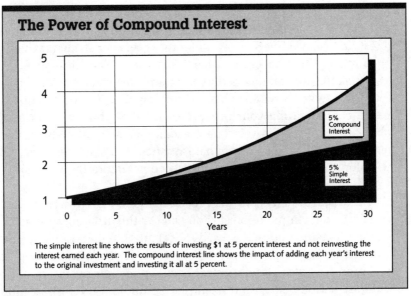

The Power of Compound Interest

The simple interest line shows the results of investing $1 at 5 percent interest and not reinvesting the interest earned each year. The compound interest line shows the impact of adding each year's interest to the original investment and investing it all at 5 percent.

CHART I

Calculating Compound and Simple Interest

Simple Interest Formula:

$$\textit{Amount invested} \times [(1 + \% \textit{ interest rate}) \times \textit{years}]$$

Compound Interest Formula:

$$\textit{Amount invested} \times (1 + \% \textit{ interest rate})^{years}$$

TABLE II

Big deal, you may be saying. One cent is not going to make much difference to my financial career. Stay tuned, though; it gets more interesting. By the end of the fifth year the difference has tripled to three cents. That is because you reinvested $1.22, earned six cents and happily turned your original dollar into $1.28, not $1.25. By the end of the eighth year the difference between compounded interest and simple interest has become eight cents, and in 10 years it is 13 cents. That's still not financial paradise, but $1.63 is better than $1.50 any day of the week.

Notice the really interesting thing about this, however. The difference gets larger each year at an accelerating pace. This can be seen most clearly on the chart. The line that shows the amount accumulated at simple interest climbs steadily in a straight line. In contrast, the line showing the amount accumulated at compound interest describes a fine soaring curve that gets ever steeper. What is happening is that the process feeds on itself. The difference between the effects of simple and compound interest, seemingly modest to start with, becomes larger and larger over time. This is because compounding your interest means that you get 5 per cent each year on a progressively larger accumulation of already earned interest in addition to your original investment. It's not very long, in fact, before the accumulated interest becomes more than the original amount.

The mathematicians call this process exponential growth, to distinguish it from simple interest. You can see the difference reflected in the mathematical formulas used for calculating the results of simple interest and compound interest in Table II. The simple-interest calculation involves straightforward multiplication by the number of interest periods, 30 in our example. Compound-interest calculations involve multiplication by the power of the number of interest periods — by the power of 30 in this case.

One implication of all this is that the more frequent the compounding, the faster the rate of increase in your savings. That is because the earlier the interest is added to the pile, the more interest is earned on the interest. For instance, if you could earn 10 per cent interest compounded annually, your dollar becomes $17.45 after 30 years. With the interest compounded monthly, that same dollar becomes $19.84. Compounded daily, it becomes $20.08. Looked at another way, after three years of annual compounding at 10 per cent, one dollar turns into $1.33. Compounded monthly, it grows to $1.35. Compounded daily, it also becomes $1.35 rounded off, but a difference will appear over a longer period of time.

Now take another look at the annual-compounding results in Table I on page 2. Notice that one dollar becomes two somewhere between the 14th and 15th year. It's approximately mid-May, actually, roughly 40 per cent of the way through the year. From this mathematical curiosity comes a handy rule of thumb, the so-called Rule of 72. This allows you to calculate in your head approximately when your money will double at a given rate of compounded annual interest. You simply divide 72 by whatever interest rate you are curious about. For example, at 10 per cent the answer is 7.2 years, at 5 per cent it is 14.4 years and at 20 per cent it is 3.6 years.

You can also see that it doesn't take too long to double your money at double-digit interest rates. The implications are enormous. Remember that accelerating curve showing exponential growth at work? If you double your money in just over 14 years at 5 per cent compounded, think how quickly you can double it in later years. The first dollar of profit takes a while, but the second dollar arrives in less than nine more years. Less than six years more and you have a profit of $3, plus your original dollar of savings.

This phenomenal acceleration is the secret behind the tale of the numerically naive king and his mathematically sophisticated teen-aged daughter who was also a whiz at checkers. The king figured the best way to ensure that his daughter would concentrate on hitting the books instead of hitting on the boys was to offer monthly prizes for scholastic achievement. He asked what his daughter wanted, and she said she wanted just one dollar placed on the first square of her checkerboard to start. The next month the king was to place double that amount — $2 — on the second square, double up to $4 on the third square the following month, up to $8 on the fourth square, to $16 on the fifth, and so on until all 64 squares received their quota.

The result was a highly motivated daughter but, before long, a bankrupt if mathematically more knowledgeable king. What he did not realize at the start was that his daughter was asking for interest of 100 per cent compounded monthly. So on the 10th square the king had to put down $512. On the 20th square the amount grew to $524,288. How much if he had kept going? The 64th square would have contained something like $9,223 trillion.

Another way to realize the significance of double-your-money, or exponential, growth is the environmentalists' trick question about the lily pond. Suppose one lily appears on the pond the first day. Then every day after that the number of new lilies doubles: two the second day, four the third day, 16 the fourth day and so on. Now suppose that it takes 20 days for the entire surface of the pond to be covered with lilies. On what day will the pond's surface be half-covered? Careful, now. It's not the tenth 10th day. The correct answer is the 19th day, because the day after that the number of lilies doubles and the pond is entirely covered.

Combine the power of exponential growth with seeking out the best available interest rate and you can do spectacularly well. Consider the Indians who received 60 guilders' worth of trinkets from

Just a Dollar a Year

Original investment		$1
Additional investment each year		$1
Total investment		$30
Annual interest		5%
Years of investing		30
Future value of total investment		$66.44

Year	Amount accumulated	Amount invested	Interest accumulated
1	$1.00	$1.00	$0.00
2	2.05	2.00	0.05
3	3.15	3.00	0.15
4	4.31	4.00	0.31
5	5.53	5.00	0.53
6	6.80	6.00	0.80
7	8.14	7.00	1.14
8	9.55	8.00	1.55
9	11.03	9.00	2.03
10	12.58	10.00	2.58
11	14.21	11.00	3.21
12	15.92	12.00	3.92
13	17.71	13.00	4.71
14	19.60	14.00	5.60
15	21.58	15.00	6.58
16	23.66	16.00	7.66
17	25.84	17.00	8.84
18	28.13	18.00	10.13
19	30.54	19.00	11.54
20	33.07	20.00	13.07
21	35.72	21.00	14.72
22	38.51	22.00	16.51
23	41.43	23.00	18.43
24	44.50	24.00	20.50
25	47.73	25.00	22.73
26	51.11	26.00	25.11
27	54.67	27.00	27.67
28	58.40	28.00	30.40
29	62.32	29.00	33.32
30	66.44	30.00	36.44

TABLE III

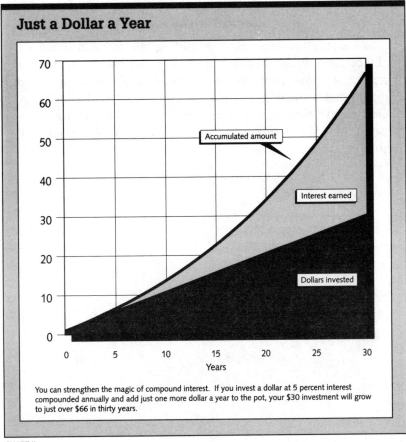

Just a Dollar a Year

Accumulated amount

Interest earned

Dollars invested

Years

You can strengthen the magic of compound interest. If you invest a dollar at 5 percent interest compounded annually and add just one more dollar a year to the pot, your $30 investment will grow to just over $66 in thirty years.

CHART II

Dutch representative Peter Minuit in 1626 for Manhattan Island, later New York. That's roughly $35 (U.S). at today's exchange rates. Had they been able to invest the money at, say, 3 per cent compounded, they would have accumulated about $1.6 billion, which is a lot of money but not enough to buy the island back. Suppose, however, they had been able to earn just 5 per cent compounded annually. It doesn't seem much of a difference, yet it increases the accumulation over 364 years to about $8.4 trillion in 1990, which would probably be enough to buy back Manhattan, at least during times of recession. What about 10 per cent compounded annually? Something like $36,000 trillion. That's what happens when you compound interest over very long periods of time.

You don't have to wait that long, or double up like the naive king, to experience gratifying profits from compounded interest. You can strengthen the magic by adding just one additional dollar to the original dollar on Jan. 1 each year and leaving everything in the pile. At 10 per cent interest (a rate we will see again someday) compounded annually, the money you invest will double in 14 years. In 20 years you will accumulate $57.27 and in 30 years $164.49. Let those figures encourage you as you begin your money-renting career.

CHAPTER 2

Money Renting Is Big Business

AT A TRUST COMPANY BRANCH in suburban Montreal, a pensioner asks for a $5,000 guaranteed investment certificate and says he will take it for five years because 7 per cent interest seems to be a good deal. On a high floor of an office tower in the Toronto-Dominion Centre, just off Toronto's famous Bay Street, a highly paid professional manager of huge amounts of other people's money offers $20 million of Government of Canada bonds for sale because she sees an opportunity to use the money more profitably in U.S. government bonds and is worried about Canada's financial prospects. In the City of London, Britain's world-renowned financial marketplace, a Canadian broker buys $20 million of EuroCanadian-dollar Government of Canada bonds and sells U.S. government bonds because he likes Canada's financial prospects and doesn't like the way things are going in the U.S. In Hong Kong, a wealthy investor moves to protect more of his assets from political and financial turmoil by picking up some Swiss-franc deposits.

All four are players in the international money-for-rent market, even though one of them probably does not know it. It's a market that dwarfs the better-known stock market. Canadian trading in the money-for-rent market amounts to several trillion dollars a year. Stock market trading is a mere $250 billion or so.

Most of the time this market operates quietly behind the scenes, with brief echoes appearing only in the financial pages and other coverage confined to specialist publications. Unlike the stock market, you cannot even watch it in action from the public gallery provided at many stock exchanges — although these days there are some corners that are visible to casual onlookers, such as the futures market in Government of Canada bonds at the Montreal Exchange.

From time to time, however, public attention swings to the money-for-rent market, usually at moments of crisis. Then you will hear breathless references on radio newscasts to what money-market traders think of the Canadian dollar. On television news you will see some of those traders talking on three telephones at once while watching rapidly changing price quotations on their video screens. Newspaper stories about what happened in the financial markets yesterday will appear on the front page instead of in the business section. Economists with acceptable communications skills and a yen for publicity will be tapped to explain what it all means.

If done properly, this media reporting and commentary will highlight how the money-market action affects people's daily lives. The connection is through the prevailing level of interest rates — in effect, how much rent is being charged or paid for the use of other people's money. As this moves up or down, so in due course do the costs of a house mortgage or a bank loan, and so do the interest rates paid on savings deposits and guaranteed investment certificates. Changes in one interest rate ripple through the money-for-rent market like wavelets on a pond.

As in any market, the going rent charged for money is determined by the changing pressures of supply and demand. When more people want to borrow other people's money than before, but the supply of money stays more or less the same, the cost of borrowing will rise. Conversely, if borrowers disappear and the supply of money looking for a profitable deal stays the same, the price charged will drop.

This is, of course, simple and easy to follow. In the real world, things do not work quite so simply. Neither supply nor demand stays more or less the same for very long. Usually they are both changing simultaneously, sometimes in the same direction and sometimes in opposite directions. There are also cross-eddies and local disturbances. As a result, disentangling the pressures that produce today's interest rates can require the skills of a good detective — and even then you usually can't be certain you have the complete picture.

Recall, for instance, those months in early 1990 leading up to the death of Canada's Meech Lake accord. This was a period in which many international investors began worrying about the political and economic stability of Canada. Some decided to sell investments in Canadian-dollar securities, such as Government of Canada bonds. This put downward pressure on Canadian bond prices, and therefore upward pressure on interest rates in general (see Chapter 9 for a detailed explanation of how bond prices work). It was not that there was suddenly more demand from borrowers for Canadian dollars, pushing up the cost of borrowing for everybody. Indeed, borrowing demand was probably weakening through this period because the economy was slowing down. Less money was being borrowed to buy houses or cars or vacation trips. It was merely a change in the attitude of some investors toward the risks of investing in Canadian dollars.

Notice also that Canadian-dollar bonds did not become pariahs in the international financial markets. Investors did not try to unload their holdings at any cost. If they had, we would have experienced what's known as a financial panic or crash, which fortunately is a rarer event than one might think. Some investors sold, but for every bond sold there was a buyer, although at a lower price. Others stood pat.

What happened was what economists call a relative change in the financial markets' rough-and-ready assessment of the balance of risks involved in owning Canadian-dollar securities. Other things being equal, Canada's convulsions over the Meech Lake accord and the internal stresses they highlighted made Canadian-dollar investments a bit riskier. Their price, therefore, had to adjust downward to offer potential buyers a larger return on their money than before. It's a process of assessment and reassessment that goes on in the financial markets for all sorts of reasons. Professional market players spend their working hours and some of their leisure hours trying to figure out what's happening and — more important if they are to take profitable advantage of their insights — what is going to happen next.

Is all this sometimes frantic activity merely a lucrative make-work project? Some critics argue it is, particularly after a market crash or the emergence of some major financial scandal. But it really isn't. Financial markets are an essential part of the system of running an economy on the basis of individual choices rather than central government planning. Like other prices throughout the economy, the varying costs of borrowing provide vital signals to all who will pay attention to what is really happening in the economy. The history of the 20th century provides countless lamentable examples of the poor results of using any other system but one based on functioning markets.

With all their imperfections, the financial markets provide the most effective way we know to transform people's savings into investments that support the economy. That is a task of importance to all of us, not just to people who have savings looking for a profitable home. Unspent money kept under a mattress does no good for anyone. Money that becomes part of the capital needed to find oil and gas, build houses and hospitals, supply supermarkets and corner stores, make movies and children's toys and manufacture airplanes and automobiles is money that is usefully employed.

In a market-based system, if demand for any of these things increases, their price will rise. This is a signal that there is probably good business to be done in increasing the supply of whatever it is that is in strong demand. In turn, that is a signal that an investment of capital in whatever is needed to increase the supply will offer a rewarding return to the source of such capital. In contrast, if some of these things fall out of favour, their price will fall. The falling price that results is a signal that capital employed in producing goods or services fewer and fewer people want would probably be better employed doing something else. As an example, consider what you can get for a black-and-white television set these days.

There can, of course, be another reason for prices to fall. The cost of producing something may have gone down permanently. Computers and other electronics products are the 20th century's prime example of this. When prices fall for this reason, the process of cause and effect will probably run the other way. Demand will rise, perhaps dramatically as in the case of electronics products, stimulating an inflow of capital into that industry. In turn, that will foster more research and development of new technology and new products providing more power at less cost.

Either way, it is important to take note of the signals that emerge from changing prices and to have a mechanism for redirecting savings efficiently. No modern industrial state operates effectively without a functioning money-for-rent market. If you participate in it, you can take modest satisfaction from knowing that in addition to earning a return on your savings, you are helping the country work.

CHAPTER 3

Knowing What Is Happening

DISCOVERING WHAT IS GOING on in the money-for-rent market is not as easy as finding out what's going on in the stock market. Except at times of financial crisis, it is rare to hear radio reports or see television news clips telling you how much bond prices rose or fell yesterday, and why. Your morning paper hardly ever publishes a detailed commentary on the money market in its business section. Even the specialist financial dailies and weeklies usually put reports about the bond market toward the back of the paper, unless something extraordinary is happening. It is almost unknown to see a column passing on a hot tip about the investment charms of a corporate debenture or warning investors of the market's dangerous overvaluation of a provincial government bond.

This, however, may be a help rather than a hindrance to the fixed-income investor. The routine daily and weekly coverage of the stock market's gyrations can overload investors with information, much of it superficial and contradictory. Facts important to an investor are there, but winnowing them from the useless chaff can be difficult and confusing.

There are two inherent reasons for this lack of publicity for day-to-day developments in the money-for-rent market. The first is that there is really only one fundamental, all-important question for the fixed-income investor: Are interest rates in general heading up, down or sideways? True, the answer to that question depends on a variety of factors and can be the subject of endless debate. But once you have reached a conclusion, the implications for the fixed-income investor are much clearer than for the stock market investor. The second reason is that working out those implications in detail for the more complicated kinds of fixed-income investments is frequently a mathematical exercise not ideally suited to be the subject of routine media coverage.

Interest rates

This survey of rates offered by a sample group of companies was prepared by Cannex Financial Exchanges, Aug. 16, 1995, at 5:01 p.m. Savings rates are non-redeemable except where indicated by an 'r'. Variable mortgage rates are open except where indicated by a 'c'. Rates are for information purposes only and should be confirmed by the company quoted.

SAVINGS RATES / MORTGAGE RATES

Company	($1,000 balance) Savings account	Chequing account	Minimum deposit	30 days	60 days	90 days	120 days	180 days	270 days	Minimum deposit	One year	Two years	Three years	Four years	Five years	Variable rate	6 month open	6 month closed	1 year open	1 year closed	2 year closed	3 year closed	4 year closed	5 year closed
BANKS																								
BCI Bank, Toronto	1.25	1.00	5,000	r3.25	r3.25	r3.25	r3.38	r3.38	r3.50	1,000	4.00	4.50	5.25	5.50	6.13	c5.50	6.50	4.95	6.88	6.13	6.75	7.38	7.70	7.95
Bank of Montreal, Toronto	2.00	0.50	5,000	3.25	3.25	3.38	3.38	3.38	3.50	1,000	4.50	4.50	5.13	5.40	6.00	c5.50	6.63	5.75	6.88	6.13	6.75	7.38	7.63	7.95
Bank of Nova Scotia, Toronto	0.25	0.25	5,000	3.25	3.25	3.38	3.38	3.38	3.63	1,000	4.50	4.50	5.13	5.40	5.85	6.00	6.63	5.75	6.88	6.13	6.75	7.38	7.75	7.95
CIBC, Toronto	0.25	0.25	5,000	3.25	3.25	3.38	3.38	3.38	3.63	1,000	4.50	4.50	5.13	5.40	6.00	6.00	6.63	5.75	6.88	6.13	6.75	7.38	7.70	7.95
Citibank, Toronto	0.50	0.50	5,000	r3.25	r3.38	r3.38	r3.38	r3.38		5,000	r4.50	r4.50	r5.13	r5.40	r6.00		6.63	5.75	6.88	6.13	6.75	7.38	7.70	7.95
HongKong Bank, Vancouver	0.50	0.50	5,000	3.25	3.25	3.38	3.38	3.38	3.38	1,000	4.63	5.13	5.13	5.40	6.00	6.00	6.63	5.75	6.88	6.13	6.75	7.38	7.70	7.95
Laurentian Bank, Montreal	0.25		10,000	3.25	3.25	3.38	3.38	3.38	3.38	1,000	4.63	5.13	5.13	5.40	6.00		6.63	5.75	6.88	6.13	6.75	7.38	7.70	7.95
National Bank of Greece, Montreal			5,000	3.38	3.38	3.50	3.63	3.63	3.63	1,000	4.75	5.38	5.38	5.75	6.25		6.63	5.75	6.88	6.88	6.88	7.50	7.75	8.00
National Bank, Montreal	0.20	0.10	5,000	3.38	3.38	3.50	3.50	3.63	3.50	1,000	4.50	5.13	5.13	5.40	6.00	6.00	6.63	5.75	6.88	6.13	6.88	7.50	7.75	7.95
Republic National Bk NY, Montreal			50,000	3.40	3.45	3.45	3.65	3.65		50,000	4.20	4.60	5.35	5.80	5.90									
Royal Bank of Canada, Montreal	0.50	0.25	5,000	3.25	3.25	3.38	3.38	3.38	3.50	500	4.50	4.50	5.13	5.40	6.00	6.00	6.63	5.75	6.88	6.13	6.75	7.38	7.70	7.95
Toronto-Dominion Bank, Toronto	1.75	0.25	5,000	3.25	3.25	3.38	3.38	3.38	3.38	1,000	4.50	5.13	5.13	5.40	5.65	6.00	6.63	5.75	6.88	6.13	6.75	7.38	7.70	7.95
TRUST COMPANIES																								
AGF Trust Co, Toronto			10,000	r3.50	4.00	4.25	4.25	4.25	4.30	1,000	4.80	5.65	5.95	6.45	6.25				6.25					
Bayshore Trust, Toronto	1.50		5,000	4.00	4.25	4.50	4.50	4.50	4.50	1,000	5.00	5.75	5.75	5.85	6.50		5.63	5.63	5.99	6.00	6.63	7.25	7.58	7.75
Bonaventure Trust, Montreal	1.50		5,000	4.00	4.38	4.50	4.38	4.50	4.50	1,000	4.75	5.13	5.50	5.88	6.25			5.75	6.00	6.13	6.75	7.38	7.70	7.95
Canada Trust, Toronto	2.00		5,000	3.25	3.25	3.25	3.38	3.50	3.50	1,000	4.75	5.50	5.50	5.88	6.25	6.00		5.75	6.75	6.00	6.75	7.25	7.58	7.75
Co-Operative Trust, Saskatoon			500	3.25	3.25	3.25	3.25	3.25	3.25	500	4.75	5.38	5.13	5.65	6.25	6.50	6.50	5.75	6.88	6.13	6.75	7.38	7.70	7.95
Effort Trust, Hamilton	1.00	1.00	5,000	3.25	3.25	3.25	3.25	3.50	3.50	5,000	5.38	5.38	5.80	6.00	6.13				6.88	6.88	7.63	7.88	8.13	8.15
Equitable Trust, Toronto			5,000	3.25	4.00	4.05	4.05	4.05	4.13	1,000	5.25	5.80	6.00	3.00	3.00				6.88	6.88	7.00	7.63	7.88	7.95
Family Trust, Markham			5,000	3.80	4.00	4.05	4.13	4.25	4.05	1,000	5.38	5.38	5.65	5.65	6.25				6.13	6.13	6.75	7.38	7.63	7.95
FirstLine Trust, Toronto			5,000	3.60	3.70	3.75	3.75	4.00	4.25	1,000	4.75	5.38	5.88	5.88	6.15	c4.95			5.75	5.75	6.64	7.27	7.49	7.95
HongKong Bank Trust, Edmonton			5,000	3.25	3.25	3.38	3.38	3.38	3.38	1,000	4.50	5.13	5.13	5.40	6.00	6.00	6.63	5.75	6.88	5.75	6.75	7.38	7.70	7.95
Investors Group Trust, Winnipeg	0.25	0.25	5,000	3.25	3.25	3.38	3.38	3.38	3.38	1,000	4.50	5.13	5.13	5.50	6.00	6.00	6.63	5.75	6.88	6.75	6.75	7.38	7.70	7.95
Montreal Trust, Montreal	1.00	0.75	5,000	3.25	3.25	3.38	3.38	3.38	3.63	500	4.50	5.13	5.13	5.65	6.25		6.63	5.75	6.88	6.13	6.75	7.38	7.70	7.95
Municipal Trust, Barrie	1.00	0.75	5,000	3.25	3.38	3.38	3.38	3.38	3.88	500	4.75	5.38	5.38	5.65	6.25	6.00	6.63	5.75	6.88	6.00	6.75	7.38	7.90	7.95
National Trust, Toronto	1.25		1,000	3.00	3.25	3.38	3.38	3.50	3.50	1,000	4.50	5.13	5.13	5.40	6.00		6.63	5.75	6.08	6.13	6.75	7.50	7.90	8.00
Peace Hills Trust, Edmonton			1,000	3.00	3.00	3.38	3.38	3.38	3.25	1,000	4.25	5.00	5.75	6.50	6.50	6.00		5.75	6.88	6.00	6.75	7.50	7.75	8.00
Peoples Trust, Vancouver			5,000	3.25	3.75	3.75	3.75	3.75	3.75	5,000	5.00	5.50	5.50	5.75	6.25				6.88	6.13	6.75	7.38	7.70	7.95
Royal Trust, Toronto	0.50		5,000	3.25	3.25	3.38	3.38	3.38	3.50	5,000	4.50	5.13	5.13	5.40	6.25	6.00	6.63	5.75	6.88	6.13	6.75	7.38	7.70	7.95
Sun Life Trust, Toronto	0.50		25,000	3.25	3.75	3.88	4.00	4.00	4.25	1,000	4.50	5.13	5.63	5.88	6.25				6.88	6.13	6.75	7.38	7.70	7.95
Trust General, Montreal			1,000	3.25	3.25	3.25	3.25	3.25	3.25	1,000	4.50	5.13	5.13	5.40	5.80		6.63	5.75	6.88	6.13	6.75	7.50	7.75	7.95
OTHER INSTITUTIONS																								
Alberta Treasury Branch, Edmonton			5,000	3.25	3.00	3.00	3.00	3.00	3.50	1,000	4.50	5.25	5.25	5.68	6.13		6.63	5.75	6.88	6.00	6.63	7.25	7.63	7.88
Arvestel Credit Union, Hamilton			5,000	3.00	3.25	3.38	3.38	3.25	3.25	1,000	4.50	5.25	5.13	5.63	6.00	8.50	6.25	5.75	6.50	6.00	6.63	7.25	7.63	7.88
CS COOP Credit Union, Ottawa			1,000	4.00	3.25	3.25	3.25	3.25	3.25	1,000	4.50	5.25	5.25	5.63	6.00	6.00	6.25	5.75	6.00	6.00	6.63	7.38	7.70	7.80
Canada Life, Toronto			1,000	r4.00	r4.00	r4.00	r4.00	r4.00	r4.00	1,000	r4.50	r4.50	r5.25	r6.00	r6.00		6.63	5.75	6.88	6.13	6.75	7.38	7.70	7.95
Capital City Savings, Edmonton	0.25	0.25	1,000	3.00	3.25	3.25	3.13	3.13	3.13	1,000	4.50	5.13	5.13	5.40	6.00	6.63		5.75	6.88	6.13	6.75	7.38	7.70	7.95
Commercial Union Life, Scarborough										10,000	r3.50	r4.90	r5.40	r5.50	r5.75									
Empire Life, Kingston										2,500	r3.75	r4.38	r5.13	r5.63	r5.88									

TABLE IV

Money rates

ADMINISTERED RATES			UNITED STATES
Bank of Canada	4.00-4.50%		NEW YORK (AP) — Money rates

ADMINISTERED RATES
Bank of Canada   4.00-4.50%
Canadian prime   6.00%
MONEY MARKET RATES
(for transactions
of $1-million or more)
3-mo. T-bill(when-issued)   4.15%
1-month treasury bills   4.03%
2-month treasury bills   4.11%
3-month treasury bills   4.15%
6-month treasury bills   4.35%
1-year treasury bills   4.63%
10-year Canada bonds   7.26%
30-year Canada bonds   7.77%
1-month banker's accept.   4.22%
2-month banker's accept.   4.23%
3-month banker's accept.   4.25%
Commercial Paper (R-1 Low)
1-month   4.26%
2-month   4.28%
3-month   4.30%
Call money   4.15%
**Supplied by Dow Jones
Telerate Canada**

UNITED STATES
NEW YORK (AP) — Money rates
for Monday as reported by Dow
Jones Telerate as of 4 p.m.:
   Telerate interest rate index:
5.340
   Prime Rate: 8.25
   Discount Rate: 5.00
   Broker call loan rate: 7.00
   Federal funds market rate:
High 5.25; low 5.1875; last 5.25
   Dealers commercial paper: 30-
180 days: 5.40-5.48
   Commercial paper by finance
company: 30-270 days: 5.28-5.33
   Bankers acceptances dealer
indications: 30 days, 5.30; 60 days,
5.30; 90 days, 5.33; 120 days, 5.32;
150 days, 5.36; 180 days, 5.36
   Certificates of Deposit Primary:
30 days, 4.46; 90 days, 4.80; 180
days, 5.01
   Certificates of Deposit by
dealer: 30 days, 5.32; 60 days, 5.35;

90 days, 5.39; 120 days, 5.44; 150
days, 5.53; 180 days, 5.55
   Eurodollar rates: Overnight,
5.125-5.25; 1 month, 5.3125-5.375; 3
months, 5.375-5.4375; 6 months,
5.5625-5.625; 1 year, 5.75-5.8125
   London Interbank Offered Rate:
3 months, 5.50; 6 months, 5.6875; 1
year, 5.875
   Treasury Bill auction results:
average discount rate: 3-month as
of Aug. 19: 5.06; 6-month as of
Aug. 19: 5.13; 52-week as of Aug.
15: 5.36
   Treasury Bill annualized rate
on weekly average basis, yield adjusted for constant maturity, 1-
year, as of Aug. 19: 5.62
   Treasury Bill market rate, 1-
year: 5.34-5.32
   Treasury Bond market rate, 30-
year: as of 4 p.m. 6.80

SOURCE: THE GLOBE AND MAIL

TABLE V

   To answer the key question of where interest rates are heading, you first need to check on where they are now. This has become much easier in recent years, largely because of the growing interest in personal money management. Many daily newspapers regularly publish sections devoted to personal finance, often once a week. Tables showing interest rates offered on fixed-income investments are common features of such sections. A representative list of financial institutions — banks, trust companies, credit unions and mortgage companies — is published, together with their rates on savings deposits and on fixed-term deposits for periods of a month or so up to five years. Checking them each week will give you a good feel for the range of rates paid and for how they are changing.

   You can also get a quick daily update on key interest rates from many daily newspapers. Check the pages in the business section, where the stock quotations and other statistical information are published, for a small table usually called "Money Markets." This table will always contain up-to-date figures for two key interest rates, the Bank of Canada rate and the prime rate. The Bank of Canada rate is a sort of official indicator of the overall direction of interest rates. It is set each day by the bank, which is a special kind of government agency that supplies banking services to the government and supervises the operation of the country's financial system.

The rate does not come out of thin air, however. It is linked to market-set interest rates, most notably the call loan rate at which the commercial banks lend money to each other overnight. The number that emerges from this process is influenced partly by general conditions in the financial markets and partly by the Bank of Canada's own ideas of what should be happening to interest rates. Once set, however, the Bank of Canada rate serves as a reference point for a multitude of other Canadian interest rates. Most notable among these is the prime rate, more fully described as the prime lending rate of the Canadian chartered banks. This is a rate used by the banks as their own reference marker for loans of all kinds to businesses and individual customers. When the prime goes up, the rates charged on other bank loans will probably go up, too — automatically in many cases and by deliberate decision, perhaps with a delay, in others.

Unlike the Bank of Canada rate, the prime is not set each day and it changes much less frequently. Typically, for example, it will take a number of small weekly increases or decreases in the Bank of Canada rate to trigger a change in the prime. The link between the two rates is indirect, through the impact of changes in the Bank of Canada rate on the cost of the huge amounts of money the banks borrow with one hand and lend to their customers with the other. Although the prime rate is higher than the Bank of Canada rate, the banks do not maintain a fixed gap between the two. The difference can vary from small to large, depending on conditions in the money-for-rent market at the time.

You should also not be surprised to see that the prime rate at all the banks is often the same. A bank that maintained a higher rate alone would eventually put itself out of the lending business. Customers would move to its lower-price rivals. From time to time a bank seeking to increase its share of the lending business may maintain a lower rate for quite a while, at the expense of its profits. But this is unlikely to be a permanent policy.

Specialist publications such as *The Globe and Mail*'s daily Report on Business supply a wide range of other current interest rates with their money market tables. You can check on the general level of U.S. interest rates and their day-to-day changes, for instance. The U.S. equivalent of the Bank of Canada rate is the discount rate,

Canadian bonds

Provided by RBC Dominion Securities

Selected quotations, with changes since the previous day, on actively traded bond issues. Yields are calculated to full maturity, unless marked C to indicate callable date. Price is the midpoint between final bid and ask quotations Aug. 19, 1996.

Issuer	Coupon	Maturity	Price	Yield	$ Chg
GOVERNMENT OF CANADA					
CANADA	8.00	15 MAR 97	102.013	4.364	+0.048
CANADA	7.00	15 SEP 97	102.425	4.642	+0.090
CANADA	6.00	15 MAR 98	101.515	4.981	+0.110
CANADA	8.00	1 NOV 98	105.185	5.456	+0.110
CANADA	5.75	1 MAR 99	100.275	5.631	+0.110
CANADA	7.75	1 SEP 99	105.145	5.869	+0.080
CANADA	8.50	1 MAR 00	107.485	6.108	+0.020
CANADA	7.50	1 SEP 00	104.284	6.279	+0.025
CANADA	7.50	1 MAR 01	104.225	6.409	+0.020
CANADA	9.50	1 OCT 01	112.675	6.539	NC
CANADA	9.75	1 DEC 01	114.096	6.543	+0.020
CANADA	8.50	1 APR 02	108.663	6.623	+0.024
CANADA	7.25	1 JUN 03	102.091	6.856	-0.037
CANADA	7.50	1 DEC 03	103.146	6.939	-0.039
CANADA	6.50	1 JUN 04	96.831	7.034	-0.038
CANADA	9.00	1 DEC 04	111.903	7.072	-0.047
CANADA	8.75	1 DEC 05	110.650	7.156	-0.050
CANADA	7.00	1 DEC 06	98.125	7.260	-0.047
CANADA	10.00	1 JUN 08	120.344	7.381	-0.080
CANADA	9.50	1 JUN 10	116.805	7.518	-0.084
CANADA	9.00	1 MAR 11	112.639	7.552	-0.083
CANADA	10.25	15 MAR 14	125.069	7.634	-0.089
CANADA	9.75	1 JUN 21	121.909	7.746	-0.113
CANADA	8.00	1 JUN 23	102.800	7.749	-0.100
CANADA	9.00	1 JUN 25	114.041	7.770	-0.111
CMHC	7.00	1 JUN 01	102.044	6.492	+0.022
REAL RETURNS	4.25	1 DEC 21	94.125	4.647	-0.100
PROVINCIAL					
ALBERTA	8.00	1 MAR 00	105.930	6.105	+0.021
ALBERTA	6.25	1 MAR 01	99.531	6.370	+0.022
ALBERTA	7.50	1 DEC 05	101.930	7.209	-0.046
B C	9.00	9 JAN 02	110.559	6.632	+0.069
B C	8.00	23 AUG 05	104.754	7.271	-0.045
B C	8.50	23 AUG 13	106.750	7.778	-0.080
B C	8.00	8 SEP 23	100.585	7.946	-0.090
B C MUN FIN	7.75	1 DEC 05	102.851	7.319	-0.046
HYDRO QUEBEC	9.25	2 DEC 96	101.325	4.349	-0.250
HYDRO QUEBEC	10.88	25 JUL 01	117.265	6.698	NC
HYDRO QUEBEC	7.00	1 JUN 04	97.935	7.351	-0.070
NEWFOUNDLAND	10.13	22 NOV 14	118.879	8.121	-0.088
NOVA SCOTIA	9.60	30 JAN 22	116.199	8.088	-0.106
ONTARIO HYD	7.25	31 MAR 98	103.385	5.025	+0.110
ONTARIO HYD	9.38	31 JAN 00	109.914	6.132	+0.017
ONTARIO HYD	9.00	24 JUN 02	110.701	6.749	+0.024
ONTARIO HYD	7.75	3 NOV 05	102.802	7.324	-0.045
ONTARIO	9.00	15 SEP 04	110.897	7.194	-0.045
ONTARIO	7.50	19 JAN 06	101.073	7.339	-0.046
ONTARIO	8.00	2 JUN 26	99.764	8.019	-0.098
P E I	9.75	30 APR 02	113.440	6.853	+0.023
P E I	8.50	27 OCT 15	104.389	8.045	-0.081
QUEBEC	8.00	30 MAR 98	104.455	5.071	+0.110
QUEBEC	10.25	7 APR 98	107.925	5.100	+0.100
QUEBEC	10.25	15 OCT 01	115.000	6.748	NC
QUEBEC	9.38	16 JAN 23	111.525	8.291	-0.150
SASKATCHEWAN	9.88	6 JUL 99	110.490	5.849	+0.073
SASKATCHEWAN	7.50	19 DEC 05	101.196	7.319	-0.045
SASKATCHEWAN	8.75	30 MAY 25	108.025	8.029	-0.100
TORONTO -MET	7.75	1 DEC 05	102.514	7.369	-0.046
CORPORATE					
AGT LIMITED	9.50	24 AUG 04	113.266	7.284	-0.046
AGT LIMITED	8.80	22 SEP 25	107.161	8.152	-0.153
AVCO FIN	8.75	15 MAR 00	107.627	6.325	+0.003
BELL CANADA	8.80	17 AUG 05	108.750	7.447	-0.048
BELL CANADA	9.70	15 DEC 32	117.490	8.184	-0.174
BC TELEPHONE	9.65	8 APR 22	116.102	8.142	-0.158
BANK OF MONT	8.15	9 MAY 11/06	104.461	7.493C	-0.047
BANK OF N S	8.90	20 JUN 25	108.240	8.152	-0.154
CENTRA GAS	8.85	1 SEP 05	108.214	7.577	-0.047
CDN IMP BANK	8.65	22 AUG 05	107.927	7.427	-0.047
CDN UTIL	8.43	1 JUN 05	107.395	7.272	-0.046
CDN UTIL	9.40	1 MAY 23	114.798	8.043	-0.160
HAMMERSON CD	8.10	21 FEB 06	100.818	7.975	-0.045
INTERPRV PIP	8.20	15 FEB 24	100.758	8.130	-0.143
MOLSON BREW	8.20	11 MAR 03	105.313	7.168	-0.037
NVA SCOT PWR	9.75	2 AUG 19	114.858	8.291	-0.149
NOVA GAS	8.30	15 JUL 03	105.939	7.190	-0.039
PANCDN PETE	8.75	9 NOV 05	108.833	7.407	-0.048

SOURCE: THE GLOBE AND MAIL

TABLE VI

which is set by the U.S. Federal Reserve Board in a somewhat different way but serves the same purpose of influencing the level of interest rates in general. There is also an equivalent U.S. version of the prime rate. The *Globe* table also contains more exotic items such as banker's acceptances, dollar swaps and brokers' call loan money. Most individual fixed-income investors do not need to understand what these might be or check what is happening to them. They are the province of the professional managers of large amounts of money working for corporations, banks and other big-time financial outfits.

Many daily newspapers with business sections also publish a regular list of price and yield quotations on marketable bonds. Bonds are sold to investors by governments and corporations to raise money. They are a sort of promissory note or receipt for borrowed money that is to be repaid eventually. In the meantime, the government or corporation pays interest on the borrowed money to whoever owns the bond. Like stocks, many such bonds can be bought and sold among investors in a huge multibillion-dollar international market known unsurprisingly as the bond market. Their price, therefore, varies from day to day as interest rates go up or down. As a result, the return on your investment (yield) if you buy one today may be different from what it was yesterday or will be tomorrow (see Chapter 9). The daily quotations tables supply the approximate price and yield for each bond listed. The actual price you pay is usually a little different, but the quoted figures give you a good idea of how bonds are faring. Some tables include more bonds than others and give additional information.

To go beyond these figures and learn what is happening in the bond and money markets in detail requires finding regularly published commentaries on the daily movements in interest rates and prices. Again, unlike the stock market, these are not found easily. Few newspapers or television or radio stations devote to these markets the kind of space or time they give to the stock market. An important exception is *The Globe and Mail*"s Report on Business, which most days publishes a commentary on the bond and money markets as well as the stock market. You will find daily international coverage of these markets in *The Wall Street Journal* and the *Financial Times* of London.

Most fixed-income investors do not need to keep in touch with daily market developments to this extent. If your money goes into government savings bonds and a term deposit or two, the day-to-day changes in the prices of market-traded bonds do not matter to you all that much. What you will find useful is a general knowledge of what is happening to interest rates now, and what seems likely to happen next. The first is, of course, a matter of fact that you can discover accurately from the various sources mentioned above. The second is a matter of opinion on which you have potentially as good a chance of being right as the professionals who spend their working hours trying to figure it out. That's because predicting the future course of interest rates, like predicting the stock market, is notoriously difficult for anybody.

It is possible to be successful both as a fixed-income investor and a stock market investor without relying on predictions of interest rates or share prices in general. Indeed, some experts recommend it. But because interest rates so totally dominate the fixed-income market, it is more difficult to avoid such predictions. You can still do very well in the stock market by buying the right shares, even if the market in general is declining. It is difficult to do that in the fixed-income markets if you are totally wrong about the probable direction of interest rates, especially if you invest in market-traded bonds. Note that it is difficult, but not impossible.

If you stick to fixed-income investments such as term deposits that you have to hold on to for a fixed period of time, why should you care about the outlook for interest rates? You cannot hope to profit in the meantime, if interest rates go down and the prices of market-traded fixed-income investments such as bonds go up, because you can't sell your term deposit to anybody else. You also need not concern yourself about the possibility that interest rates will go up, and bond prices down, because your term deposit will still retain its full value and be repaid in full when it matures.

There is a reason, though. It is precisely because of the fact that when you buy a term deposit or a guaranteed investment certificate, you are renting your money out for a fixed period of time, varying from months usually up to five years. That's a serious commitment. In many cases you can't get your money back at all before the time is up. In other cases, you will receive a very low rate of investment if you cash in early, and sometimes no interest at all. It's entirely up to you to choose how long and that choice amounts to an investment decision, whether it is made consciously or not.

Suppose you decide on a five-year deal at 7 per cent. Then suppose that interest rates go down over the next year or so. You will feel pretty good because your 7 per cent is locked in for five years while people who went for, say, a one-year deal are getting their money back and reinvesting it at, say, 5 per cent. In addition, by the time your money is looking for a new home in five years, rates may be back up to 7 per cent or more.

But suppose that, far from going down after you make your five-year arrangement, interest rates climb instead. Now you are the one who is sitting with a lousy 7 per cent while the people who made short-term deals are reinvesting for 12 per cent or more. Better keep your day job, after all.

From all this come two basic rules of fixed-income investing:

- If interest rates go down, you will do better with a longer-term deal you make today.
- If interest rates go up, a short-term deal made today will be more rewarding.

During the long upward climb to record high interest rates in the final years of the 1970s, people who lent their money out for short periods of time did well. During the decline from those peaks in the early years of the 1980s, people who had the wit and the courage to make long-term deals did even better. Like many things, it's a question of timing.

Note that if you are the borrower, not the lender, it's the other way round. A long-term borrower at today's rate is sitting pretty if interest rates rise, at least until the loan has to be renegotiated, but a short-term borrower may be in trouble. If interest rates fall, however, that same long-term borrower will feel sick and the short-timer will be happy. It's always important to remember who is doing the borrowing and who is lending.

How do you go about handling this decision? The best way is to avoid it by never being a hero. Even though you are totally convinced that interest rates are going down over the next few years, you never rent your money out for more than, say, 10 years, and you invest some money for just one year, in case you are wrong. Again, even if you think interest rates are bound to go higher in the next little while, you don't take the shortest-term deal available. You hedge your bet by committing some money for several years, in case you are wrong. If you have substantial savings, you can spread the money around for several different periods of time—some in short-term deals and the rest in longer-term commitments. This way you will never be gloriously right, but neither will you be painfully wrong. It's the best approach for those who don't want to spend much time following the continuous debate among the experts over future interest rates.

Those who prefer a more active approach must pay enough attention to that debate to reach some conclusion of their own. They should also keep their eyes open to see what is going on in the world around them. Remember that the level of interest rates fundamentally reflects the balance of supply and demand for borrowed money. If everything around you says we are in booming economic times, the odds are that interest rates are rising because borrowing demand will be strong. If, on the contrary, everything indicates we are in an economic slowdown, the odds are that interest rates, or the price of borrowed money, are falling. Note, however, that this is a matter of probabilities, not certainties. There are always special circumstances to be taken into account.

You may find some basic reporting of the debate in the business section of your local daily newspaper. But these reports, where they exist, are frequently too brief to provide much guidance. For more adequate coverage you will have to tackle *The Globe and Mail*"s Report on Business or a specialist financial weekly such as *The Financial Post*. Television programs concentrating on the world of business may also be useful. Again, for international coverage you will need *The Wall Street Journal* or the *Financial Times* of London.

The larger investment dealers have full-time analysts, usually economists, who are paid to peer into the future and assess which way interest rates will move. Their work is principally aimed at professional money managers of large amounts of other people's money, who can throw large amounts of commission business the firm's way in payment for the advice. But if you are a client of the firm, you may have some access to their comments through your broker. The views of these interest-rate gurus are also frequently reported in media coverage of the interest-rate outlook.

These interest-rate analysts spend a lot of their time studying the business cycle. Modern industrial economies have delivered material living standards beyond the dreams of earlier ages and of many of the world's people even today. Yet most of us are aware that things don't always go smoothly. Like life, the economy has its ups and downs. A complete sequence of up and down makes one cycle. The encouraging thing is that over reasonable periods of time, we usually cycle in an upward direction. In other words, the starting point of each cycle is generally higher than the starting point of the previous cycle.

The size of a country's economy is measured by what economists call the gross domestic product, which is the dollar value of all goods and services the country produces. If that figure increases from one year to the next, the country's economy is said to be growing. Note that this does not necessarily mean every individual in the country is better off. It just means the total production of goods and services, measured in dollar terms, is up. Note also that in these inflationary times, when a dollar buys less this year than last, only real economic growth is counted. This is done by excluding from the calculation those increases in the gross domestic product that result purely from increases in the prices of goods and services.

If you plot annual gross domestic product figures on a chart, you will see both the long-term upward trend and the continual interruptions. Exactly why industrial economies show this pattern is hotly debated. If we knew for sure, we could perhaps do something to moderate the impact of the downdrafts on people's daily lives. The business cycle is one of those things that is much easier to explain after the fact than to divine while it is happening. It is even more difficult to predict what is going to happen next, from which comes the veteran economist's advice to a newcomer to the trade: Forecast cautiously and often.

One reason for this is that economic statistics such as the gross domestic product and the inflation rate are only approximations. As a result, they are almost always revised as new information comes in. They are also always out of date. At best, the picture they give is like the one a driver sees in her rearview mirror. She can get a pretty good idea of where she has been, but that doesn't tell her for sure what's around the next bend.

Don't be too disheartened, though. To rent your money out profitably and safely, which is the goal of the fixed-income investor, it is not necessary to become an expert in these areas. The important thing is to have a sense of approximately where we are in the current economic cycle. That will give you a feel for whether the demand for borrowed money is increasing, decreasing, or staying more or less the same.

For the more daring, the really big opportunities occur late in each phase of the cycle, before it changes direction. Just before boom changes to slowdown, interest rates will usually be at their highest point. Renting out your money for a long period at those rates will seem a very smart idea later on when the available interest rates are much lower. Again, just before slowdown gives way to renewed economic expansion, interest rates will usually be at their lowest point. It would therefore be a smart move to rent your money out for short periods of time, and be able to re-rent it at successively higher interest rates as the demand for borrowed money rises.

How do you decide whether we are at one or other of those points in time? You can read everything you can find on the continuing debate on the economy. Or you can consult experts on the subject. In the end, however, the conclusion is up to you — and it is not an easy one to reach. If it were easy, we could all be rich or, more practically, the financial markets just wouldn't work. It is because reasonable people differ about future prospects that borrowers and lenders can mutually agree on the interest rate to be paid on a particular deal, just as buyers and sellers agree on a price in the stock market. One side or the other will turn out to be wrong, but at the time the deal is done, both believe they are doing the smart thing. On such touching faith any market rests.

CHAPTER 4

Watch for Those Con Men

IF IT SOUNDS TOO GOOD TO be true, it probably is. Michael Milken, former bond trader, con man extraordinaire and self-confessed white-collar crook, taught us that lesson once again during the 1980s. Anyone who rents money out in any of the many possible ways described in this book should never forget it, whatever the temptation.

On March 3, 1991, Milken reported to a federal prison camp in Pleasanton, Calif., to begin serving a 10-year sentence for committing one of the most highly publicized financial industry crimes in history.

The seemingly remarkable thing about this event was not that a professional investor had been exposed and punished as a crook. The investment business, like all other occupations, has always had its share of lawbreakers. What was seen as remarkable was that Milken had arrived at this point by way of a career in trading and selling bonds. It is usually the stock market, not the bond market, that is considered a promising arena for relieving investors of their money in criminal ways. Stocks, no matter how mundane or insubstantial the business of the companies involved, always offer the allure of big money made quickly. But bonds? Renting your money out safely for regular interest payments and the eventual return of every cent of the loan? How can that dull business become the stuff of a huge financial scandal?

Well, it has before, and it was once again. Milken based his con game on the sale to eager investors of so-called junk bonds. You might ask why anybody would pay good money for self-described junk. But you might also wonder why 17th-century European investors paid fortunes for tulip bulbs. Why did 18th-century British investors hand over good money for shares in a company that said it would use the funds in a profitable business, with "nobody to know what it is"? And why did 20th-century U.S. investors buy fraudulent company bonds with their eyes shut merely because famous names were attached to them. The answer: a poisonous mix of a spellbinding spinner of tales and the greed that lurks in all of us.

Milken spun a tale about bonds that offer an unusually high yield. Remember that the normal rule of thumb is that the higher the yield, the greater the risk. Poorly rated borrowers have to pay more interest than top-rated borrowers. There was a good reason why these bonds were called junk bonds. That's what many of them, perhaps most, were. Yet Milken promised customers that if they bought a diversified portfolio of junk bonds they would do better than by sticking to dull lower-yield bonds.

On the face of it this seems unlikely, but there is just enough plausibility to it to give a con man a handhold. If you pick your high-yield bonds carefully and watch them like a hawk, you might be able to turn the odds in your favour. It's not easy, but it's possible. Some stock market investors do pretty well using the same technique to buy the shares of promising smaller companies. They still lose money on their mistakes, but what they win on the occasional big successes makes up for that.

This was not what Milken wanted the customers to do. There aren't that many high-yield bonds of promising companies around to make selling them to investors possible on a big scale. So Milken and his henchmen did three key things:

They took an obscure and tentative academic theory of finance and dressed it up to look like a universal law of the market: You can't go wrong buying high-yield junk bonds, especially if you buy them from experts like Milken and company. Their rate of default is not much greater than that of triple-A bonds, they said.

They made sure there was a huge supply of new junk bonds to be sold then traded, so that big-dollar professional investors could say there was enough liquidity to get them out of a deal if it turned sour.

They made sure there appeared to be a thriving market for the stuff by putting together a network of eager buyers and sellers who would pass the low-value, high-yield bonds among themselves at essentially rigged prices.

Like any such scheme, the early investors got paid by those who came in later. A chain letter works the same way. It also has the same fundamental problem: To keep things going, the con man has to bring in an ever-increasing number of new investors. Milken's evil genius was that he was able to keep the junk bond scam going immeasurably longer and on a bigger scale than anybody would believe if they hadn't seen it.

To do so, he made common cause with financial raiders. They borrowed huge amounts of money through his junk bonds to launch an oft-repeated parody of corporate takeovers in which the interest and money were to be repaid by looting the treasury and selling the assets of the target company. Some of the early deals of this kind, so-called leveraged buyouts, made business sense. But not for long. In the early 1990s, the U.S. corporate landscape was littered with the corpses and the crippled casualties of these campaigns. As with any financial craze, the bad deals drove out the good.

When much deeper pockets were needed, Milken and the Wall Street firm he dominated from his California office, Drexel Burnham Lambert, joined forces with a whole slew of executives of U.S. savings and loan companies, and ultimately life insurance companies, to have them buy junk bonds. There is now a long list of these companies whose finances were ruined by their purchases of junk bonds, and U.S. taxpayers are on the hook for hundreds of billions of dollars of losses. The junk bond scam helped put the stability of the entire U.S. financial system in question by the end of the 1980s.

The sheer scale of the junk bond debacle might seem to put it in a class of its own, but fundamentally it isn't unique. Milken and his cronies used no trick or manoeuvre that hadn't been used by con men before. Seemingly solid evidence of something that is contrary to common sense reappears distressingly often in financial history. In a competitive market there is no way in which the theory behind junk bond investing advanced by Milken could remain true for long, if it ever was. No above-market rate of return on investments supposedly posing the same level of risk can survive for long because of the natural reaction of alert investors to profit from it by buying. That buying raises the price and lowers the return.

Junk bonds are junk bonds and triple-A bonds are triple-A bonds. No incantation by Michael Milken or a whole faculty of finance professors can change the fact that the former are riskier than the latter. True, some junk bonds may change into triple-A bonds and some triple-A bonds may become junk bonds. That's no surprise. It's a costly mistake for investors to let themselves believe they are the same thing.

The junk bond scam of the 1980s is over, although not its consequences. You must always remember, though, that there will be
other scams. They won't seem like scams when they begin; they
will probably sound like a brilliant new way to beat the basic odds
of the game. So there is only one person who can protect you from
falling victim to one: yourself. Watch for the tipoffs in the sales
pitch. Some red-flag phrases:

- "It's easy to get rich quick this way."
- "You just can't lose on this one."
- "This one is selling out fast, so you'd better get in now."
- "Would the government give you a tax break if it wasn't a safe
investment?"

Above all, always ask yourself this mind-concentrating question:
If this deal is so good, why are they going to such great lengths to let
me in on it?

CHAPTER 5

Building a Stake

TO HAVE SOME SURPLUS money to rent out you need to have saved some first. This is not at all easy, as legions of people whose spending always matches or exceeds their income can testify. How to accumulate some unspent cash is the theme of other books. (For example, see *The Money Companion*, another title in The Globe and Mail Personal Finance Library.) There are many ways to do it. A savings account at a bank, trust company or credit union is where it can all begin; not only can you build a nice starting stake, you get paid for it, too. The trick is to avoid paying the bank, trust company or credit union for the privilege of lending your money to it.

You might think opening a savings account would be a snap, and you would be right. Surplus money is the raw material of banks and their competitors, the other financial institutions. They are in business principally to lend it to their customers for a higher rent than they paid for it. Just walk into any branch, answer a few routine questions to identify yourself, hand over some cash or a cheque, and an account will be opened for you just as quickly as the information can be entered into the computer.

You might also think it would be simple and uncomplicated — but you would be wrong. The first decision that may perplex you is choosing the kind of account you require. "What do you have?" you will probably ask, unsuspecting. Then may come the deluge. "Will that be our premium gold savings account that pays you super-high interest once you put more than $50,000 into it?" "You don't have $50,000? Well, then, perhaps you would prefer our investment savings account, which pays interest on every dollar except the first $600 and doesn't cost you anything to write a cheque so long as you keep more than $600 in it and so long as you don't want your cheques returned to you each month?"

"You just want a regular savings account? Sure. We've got one where withdrawing your money won't cost you a thing so long as you keep at least $1,000 in there for the entire calendar month. Otherwise, it will cost you $1.40 for each withdrawal after the first two, which are free. Of course, you get interest only on the lowest balance during the month, so if you clear out the account to pay all your bills on the last day, you may owe us instead of us owing you. The interest rate? Why, it's competitive, naturally."

And so on, and so on. By the time you're through, you may just decide to go and spend the money instead. There are signs of a growing revolt among customers against this complicated bazaar, however, and some financial institutions have begun offering deliberately simple choices. If this works in the marketplace, it may spread and the job of choosing a savings account will become easier. However, you should still know your way through the thickets and ambushes laid for unwary savers by some institutions, in case you happen to walk into one. Remember that a financial institution is not a charity; it is a business. The less it has to pay you for its raw material, the happier its managers will be. If you end up paying it for using your money, they will be ecstatic. Regard it as one of life's minor challenges to disappoint your financial institution, if you can.

The first crucial point to remember is that the quoted interest rate is not always what it seems. You can't just pick out the highest number and leave it at that. You should find out two things that can make a big difference: the basis of the calculation and how often interest is paid.

In the bad old days the banks had it all their own way. They kindly offered you a personal savings account on which they paid a low annual interest rate. The amount of interest earned was calculated monthly on the lowest balance in the account during that month. If the balance dropped to zero for a single day, the bank did not have to pay any interest at all. Worse, the bank did not actually pay you the interest each month. It was put into your account only twice a year, usually at the end of April and the end of October. This meant that you could not start to earn interest on the interest until then, assuming you did not spend it right away. In other words, the interest was compounded only semi-annually. Remember, money grows faster the more frequently it is compounded.

This was a great deal for the banks. They got to use your money for long periods of time at a minimum cost, sometimes for no rent at all. The amazing thing was how long they got away with it. One reason was a legal interest-rate ceiling of 6 per cent on how much a bank could charge, which was abolished only in 1967. This contributed to a lack of competition because rival institutions such as trust companies found it tough to grow within the legal constraint on interest. Another reason was the lack of computers to handle more frequent interest calculations.

The logjam was broken with the first daily-interest savings accounts offered by aggressive trust companies and by the growing numbers of credit unions. On these accounts the quoted interest rate was still an annual rate, but it was calculated on a daily basis, using the balance in the account at the end of each day. This meant that even if your balance was zero for a day or more, you still earned interest for the other days when there was something in the account. Note that the interest was not compounded daily. The amount earned was paid into the account sometimes just twice a year, which gave you semi-annual compounding like a regular savings account. However, for competitive reasons some institutions soon began offering monthly compounding by paying the interest into your account each month.

Clearly, a daily-interest account is a much better deal for people whose savings accounts fluctuate a lot from constantly depositing and withdrawing money. It takes a big difference in interest rates to offset the impact of earning no interest at all for a whole month or more. Monthly compounding is also a better deal if the interest rate stays the same — which, of course, it doesn't. The trade-off for the greater flexibility of a daily-interest account is always a lower interest rate. One of the few certainties in this business is that you never get something for nothing.

Another certainty is that it takes a surprisingly small difference in the interest rate to offset completely the advantage of monthly compounding over semi-annual compounding. At interest rates up to about 11 per cent, the standard differential of a quarter of a percentage point always works out in the financial institution's favour. Above that level, up to about 13.75 per cent, it takes only a discount of three-eighths of a percentage point.

Still, the introduction of the daily-interest account was a boon to customers, many of whom never earned any interest with the previously available type of account. Those who really worked at it could keep all their money in a daily-interest account, withdrawing cash or transferring it to a chequing account only on the day when it was needed and as often as necessary. That way, interest earnings would be maximized at the cost of paying close attention. It was fun while it lasted, but it wasn't too long before the financial institutions caught on. Their solution was withdrawal fees, charged once a fixed and small number of withdrawals had taken place in a single month. After you used up your free allowance, you started paying to get your own money back.

A commonly encountered variation that takes most of the fun out of daily-interest savings accounts these days is the combination of a minimum balance rule plus withdrawal fees. Meet the required minimum each month and you don't get charged for withdrawing your own money. If you don't succeed in doing that, you may still get two withdrawals a month free of charge but after that you pay up. In some cases, if your balance drops below, say, $200 during a month, you get charged a monthly fee even if you don't touch the account at all. You may find this bizarre, but there it is.

All of this web of rules and requirements is designed to encourage customers to behave the way financial institutions most like you to behave: Put lots of money into a savings account and keep it there. The bane of a banker's life is the customer who opens a savings account, then keeps putting money in and taking it out in small amounts. This is not a totally unreasonable attitude. It does cost money for financial institutions to open and administer accounts, although perhaps not as much as their spokespersons maintain.

The principal carrot offered for keeping a lot of money in a savings account today is the so-called "tiered" interest-rate scheme. In its clearest form, the institution offers a graduated scale of higher rates on larger balances. The portion of your balance below $3,000 might earn one rate, the portion between $3,000 and below $10,000 would earn a higher rate, and so on. Under this arrangement, your cash earns the interest rate for the tier in which it falls. For example, the interest on a particular day's closing balance of $21,000 might be a blend of four rates. Try working it out in your head or with pencil and paper and you can see that this sort of thing could only be done on a large scale with the aid of computers.

There are some tricky points to watch if you have enough money to qualify for the tiered rates. Check to see that you still get some interest even if your balance drops to a small amount from time to time. Some accounts don't pay any interest on a balance below a certain amount. More generously, some pay the highest applicable rate on all the money in the account, not just on the top tier. Make sure also that the interest is calculated on each day's balance, not on the smallest balance during a month. It should be paid each month to give you the benefit of monthly compounding.

There is a bigger question, too. Why use even these tiered savings accounts for long-term savings? Once you have accumulated at least $1,000 that you do not expect to have to spend in the next little while you can almost always do better by putting it into a term deposit or a guaranteed investment certificate.

Savings accounts are for short-term savings. You can use them most smartly this way. It's probably best to keep things as simple as possible. You could use a basic chequing account to pay your bills, transferring the money needed each month from a daily-interest savings account but staying within the free-withdrawal allowance if at all possible. For many of us, however, this might be tricky because it requires you to estimate fairly accurately how much money to transfer. Otherwise you will end up paying fat fees merely to get at your own money. A compromise solution is to use a combination chequing and savings account for your day-to-day needs, but make sure it is a daily-interest account.

At the end of each month, you then transfer whatever amount you can set aside for longer-term savings to a regular savings account. So long as it remains untouched, this money will earn a higher interest rate than if you left it in the daily-interest account. When the amount of money in this account grows to $1,000 or more, you shop the market for a term deposit or a guaranteed investment certificate and go on from there. Make sure you withdraw the money from the account early in a new month, not on the last day of the previous month. That will ensure you do not lose a full month's interest merely because of bad timing.

Of course, the highest promised interest rate means nothing if you don't actually get paid any. Worse still, suppose you don't get your savings back at all because the institution has gone bust. Happily, a government-backed insurance scheme provides effective protection against the consequences of such a calamity. Nationally, it is run by a federal agency called the Canada Deposit Insurance Corporation (CDIC). If you look around your local bank branch, you should see the corporation's membership sign displayed some-where.

Not all financial institutions are members of CDIC. The privilege is limited to banks, trust companies and loan companies. If they are federally incorporated, membership is automatic throughout the country. Provincially incorporated institutions can apply to the CDIC for membership, and many do. Quebec goes a slightly different way: It operates a separate deposit insurance scheme for institutions incorporated in that province, mostly caisses populaires — Quebec's brand of credit unions — and some trust companies. The rules of the Quebec Deposit Insurance Board are, in all important respects, the same as the federal rules.

You don't pay directly for the insurance protection. Member institutions are assessed fees for the coverage. The key number to remember is $60,000. That is the total amount of insurance protection any individual saver has on all deposits made at all branches of a single institution — with some exceptions, such as registered retirement savings plan deposits — covering both principal and interest. So if you deposit $60,000 at one branch of the Royal Bank of Canada and then deposit another $60,000 at another branch of the same bank down the street, and the Royal goes bust, your total coverage under the insurance scheme will be $60,000, not $120,000. However, if you deposited the second $60,000 at a branch of Canada Trust and both institutions went bust, your whole $120,000 would be covered. Let's hope such a double calamity never occurs, however, because there is some doubt that the CDIC or the country would be able to afford it.

There are other ways to boost your coverage at a single institution. You can deposit $60,000 in your spouse's name and it will be protected. Then you put another $60,000 into a joint account and get protection for that. Registered retirement savings plans are considered separate accounts from your ordinary savings accounts, too, so you can get a total of $60,000 protection at a single institution on money deposited in them. Be careful with RRSPs, though. The insurance covers only deposits that qualify under the CDIC rules — not stock market investments or mortgages, for instance.

Note that only Canadian-currency deposits are covered. Here is a list of the principal varieties of deposits eligible for protection:

- Savings and chequing accounts
- Term deposits

- Guaranteed investment certificates maturing in five years or less
- Money orders and certified drafts or cheques
- Travellers' cheques issued by member institutions

What the government insurance protection gives you is mostly peace of mind, unless you happen to be among the handful of Canadians caught now and then with money in a failed institution. Stay within the necessary limits and you can deposit your savings in the newest and smallest trust company in the country with reasonable safety and obtain the highest possible return, so long as it is a member of the CDIC or Quebec's equivalent. There is, however, a more subtle risk you take in just seeking out the highest possible return. The government insurance covers interest earned only up to the time of default. Suppose you had put your money away for five years at a good rate. Then you collect on the insurance one year later and interest rates have fallen. You will get your money back, plus one year's interest at the original rate. But now you will have to reinvest at lower rates. Note that you must allow for any interest earned when you apply the $60,000 cutoff. If you have $59,500 deposited and are owed $1,000 of interest, only $500 of the interest will be refunded by the government.

This arrangement may be bad for the financial system because it rewards financial entrepreneurs who take big risks with their customers' money, but there is no denying it can be equally rewarding for savers who know what they are doing. It may still be worthwhile, however, for you to spread your savings around among some big, well-established institutions as well. Your nerves will probably feel less strain, if nothing else.

CHAPTER 6

Canada Savings Bonds: A Good Start

ONCE A YEAR, THE CANADIAN government offers fixed-income investors a deal that's worth close consideration. The sale each fall of Canada Savings Bonds provides an opportunity for an almost perfect investment, especially for beginners. That's mainly because the government is a borrower on the grand scale, and like all borrowers in such a situation it has to offer good terms to get the money it needs. In mid-1996, Ottawa owed about $30 billion to owners of its savings bonds, roughly 5 per cent of its total debt of some $600 billion.

When you buy a Canada Savings Bond you get a nicely printed piece of paper that records your loan and sets out the government's promise to repay the money on a certain date "or on demand at the owner's option." Those last seven words are one of the two key characteristics of the savings bonds. They mean that, unlike most other bonds and many other fixed-income investments, you can turn them in on any business day you like, except for a month or two after the initial purchase, and get your money back in full.

The quid pro quo for this unusual opportunity is that you cannot sell your bonds to anybody else. They are issued and registered in the name of the original buyer. This procedure helps protect you against loss, theft or destruction of your bonds. Only individual Canadian residents, plus resident estates and trusts for individuals, qualify to buy them. No companies need apply, and there is a maximum purchase limit set for each year's sale (the 1995 limit was $100,000). However, owners of previous issues maturing at the time can usually reinvest all the face value of their expired bonds in the new issue on top of the annual limit.

In other words, the savings bonds are not at all the same thing as marketable government bonds traded in financial markets. They do not go up or down in price and you have no hope of a capital gain or fear of a capital loss if you buy them. Your only real loss would occur if the rate of interest paid, after tax, was less than the rate of inflation experienced during the time you own the bonds.

As with any investment, you could also suffer from lost opportunities in other higher-paying investments. However, it's easier to switch out of savings bonds into something else than out of most other things. You always get the full face value of the savings bonds, plus in most cases the interest owing up to the end of the month before the one in which you cash in. So it's a good idea always to cash in early in the month. There is one exception: If you cash in within a few months of the Nov. 1 issue date, you do not get any interest. In 1995, for instance, the no-interest deadline was Jan. 31, 1996. Cash in after that deadline, though, and your interest is calculated in full from Nov. 1. This rule was introduced to discourage large-scale speculation in years when savings bonds are an especially good deal for the buyer, and to limit the government's commission expenses for money raised for only a brief period. Ottawa pays 0.625 per cent of sales to distributors of the bonds.

Canada Savings Bonds go on sale during October. They usually have to be paid for on Nov. 1, but the work involved in handling the massive distribution means you don't usually receive the bonds for another month or so. The government can and does stop the sale of a particular issue at any time. This has occurred as early as Oct. 30, with the 1987 series, and as late as the following summer for the 1980 series. Sales of the 1995 series, which initially paid 5.25 per cent, ended Nov. 1, 1995. The cutoff date chosen depends on how attractive the bonds are in any particular year in relation to other comparable fixed-income investments and how much money the government wants to raise this way. Ottawa's money-raisers balance the need for cash to cover the government's financial deficit against the drawbacks. The savings bonds are an expensive way to borrow and the money can flow out as fast as it came in. In fact, the government temporarily raised the annual rate on the 1994 bonds and on all other previous issues to 6.5 per cent for May through July, 1995, to stop an outflow.

The odds used to be very much against the government and in favour of buyers of savings bonds. Ottawa is always obliged to pay whatever interest rate is necessary at the time of sale to raise the money it wants. That's why it was forced to offer a memorable 19.5 per cent in 1981. At one time, the initial rate was fixed for the life of a particular issue, typically seven to 10 years. Effectively, this rate worked as a floor but not a ceiling. If interest rates on other comparable investments rose, the government was eventually obliged to raise the return on its savings bonds, too. If interest rates on other comparable investments fell, the government was left paying higher-than-average rates on its bonds.

Ottawa improved the odds in its favour by offering the going interest rate for the first year only and by setting a minimum rate for succeeding years at well below that rate. In 1987, it eliminated the minimum rate for succeeding years entirely. The interest rate the government paid on previous years' issues was announced each fall when the terms of the new issue were announced. This effectively turned investing in the savings bonds into a one-year deal for the buyer, and made them less attractive. However, with the fall of 1994 issue, Ottawa decided to reinstate guaranteed minimum rates for the first three years. Moreover, it set successively higher minimum rates for the second and third years.

You can choose to receive your interest in one of two ways: paid annually, or only when you cash in your bonds. Buy a regular-interest savings bond and you get an interest cheque from the government each Nov. 1. You can also arrange to have the money deposited directly into your bank account. If you redeem a regular-interest bond in September and October, an amount equivalent to the interest you aren't entitled to is deducted from the full face value. But a full year's interest is sent to you Nov. 1. In effect, the government closes the books at the end of August in order to prepare the Nov. 1 cheques for distribution.

You can buy this type of savings bond only for cash, not on credit through a payroll savings scheme. They come in face amounts of $300, $500, $1,000, $5,000 and $10,000. Choosing the right denominations is important at cash-in time because you can't do partial redemptions. In other words, you can't turn in a $5,000 bond and ask for change of $4,900. You can swap your regular-interest bonds for compound-interest bonds of the same series up to Aug. 31 after the issue date.

Compound-interest savings bonds, as their name implies, encourage people to take advantage of the power of compound interest. Instead of cashing annual interest cheques, you leave the interest with the government to compound annually. The result is that after the first year, you earn interest on the interest. When you cash in, you

Comparison of Regular and Compound Interest Savings Bonds

$1,000 Series S50 issue, Nov. 1, 1995
(assuming first-year 5.25% rate and minimum rates for years two and three maintained

Total interest:

Regular interest bond	$180.00
Compound interest bond	$190.96

	1996*	1997*	1998*
Regular interest bond			
Principal	$1,000.00	$1,000.00	$1,000.00
Interest	52.50	60.00	67.50
Total	$1,052.50	$1,060.00	$1,067.50
Compound interest bond			
Principal	$1,000.00	$1,052.50	$1,115.65
Interest	52.50	63.15	75.31
Redemption value	$1,052.50	$1,115.65	$1,190.96

*on Nov. 1
+5.25% through October, 1996; minimum 6% second year; minimum 6.75% third year.

TABLE VII

collect the full face amount of your bonds plus all the interest accrued to the end of the immediately preceding month.

Table VII shows how this works. It indicates, for instance, what happens to a buyer of compound-interest bonds from the 1995 issue if he cashes his bonds two years later and three years later, assuming the average first-year interest rate of 5.25 per cent is maintained and minimum rates announced for second and third years are paid. After two years he would get $1,115.65, of which $1,000 would be the original investment and $115.65 would be interest. After two years with a regular-interest bond a purchaser would have earned just $112.50 interest, a difference of $3.15. At the two-year mark the difference in interest earned on the two types of bond would widen to $10.96.

Naturally, the taxman wants his cut of the interest paid on both types of savings bond. Income tax is payable according to the normal rules (see Chapter 18) on regular-interest cheques for the year you receive the money. With the compound-interest option, you have a limited choice of how to pay taxes. For such bonds acquired before 1990 you can include the amount earned each year in your income and pay tax due on it, even though you have not actually received the money. Alternatively, you can defer paying the tax, but only for a little while. You must pay for the year you actually collect your interest. You must also include the amount of compound interest earned in your income at least once every three years. However, for such bonds acquired after 1989, you can no longer defer paying tax on the interest you haven't received. You must declare and pay tax on it each year. There is another catch, too. Once you have made your choice, you must stick to it in following years when reporting interest earned on any similar securities, not just the particular savings bonds concerned.

Compound-interest savings bonds come in denominations as small as $100, and range up to $10,000 in the same steps as regular-interest bonds. This smaller minimum amount makes them ideal for beginning a savings program. They are also more flexible because you can swap them for regular-interest bonds of the same series at any time until they mature.

Compound-interest savings bonds are also the only type eligible for payroll savings plans, which are highly useful devices for encouraging personal savings. If you work for an employer that offers one of these schemes, each fall you will be offered the chance to sign up for as many of the new-issue savings bonds as you want, within reason. You pay for the bonds through payroll deductions by your employer. These deductions cover the full amount, plus interest, over 12 months. At the end of the 12 months you receive your fully paid-for bonds. In effect, you borrow the money from your employer's bank, which is why you have to pay interest.

The beauty of the scheme is twofold. First, there is the psychological reinforcement it offers. Once you have committed yourself, the money to pay for the bonds is deducted from your pay automatically. This means that, like all those other deductions, you don't have to make a conscious decision to set the money aside. True, you can cancel the arrangement at any time if you need to and get all your money back, but few people do so. Second, even though you don't actually get your hands on your bonds until a year later, you start earning interest right away, just like any normal purchaser. Because the interest charged on your loan is the same rate as the inter-

Canada Savings Bonds and Their Maturity Dates

Series No.	Issued (Nov. 1)	Mature (Nov. 1)	Interest (%)	Minimum (%)
S42	1987	1997	6.37	*
S43	1988	1998	6.37	*
S44	1989	2001	6.37	*
S45	1990	2002	6.37	*
S46	1991	2003	6.37	*
S47	1992	2004	6.37	*
S48	1993	2005	6.37	*
S49	1994	2006	6.37	*
S50	1995	2007	5.25	†

*6.75% beginning Nov. 1, 1995; 7.5% beginning Nov. 1, 1996
†6% beginning Nov. 1, 1996; 6.75% beginning Nov. 1, 1997

TABLE VIII

est paid on your bonds, you come out even. It's a pretty sweet deal and many Canadians have used it to start building their savings.

Banks and other financial institutions used to offer instalment payment schemes for savings bonds on similar terms, but these have been discontinued. However, there is nothing to stop you from borrowing to buy a new issue of savings bonds. What you do is make a deal with your bank or trust company to borrow the cash and buy the bonds in the normal way. As security for the loan, you hand over your newly purchased bonds, which should get you a favourable interest rate, although it is unlikely to be low enough for the interest you earn on the bonds to offset it entirely. If you don't make the payments as agreed, you lose the bonds to the lender. If you do live up to the deal, you get your bonds out of hock and emerge free and clear. The psychological reinforcement in such an arrangement is almost as strong as from buying through a payroll plan. Nobody likes to default on a loan after committing themselves to it.

Savings bonds are, in general, very acceptable security for loans, likely to win you the best available interest rate. That's because their value never declines, unlike marketable bonds and stocks. They are always worth 100 cents on the dollar, plus accrued but unpaid interest. Clearly, you should not use savings bonds that form part of your emergency cash reserve as collateral for loans. That is an unacceptable risk. But the effective use of savings bonds to leverage your fixed-income investments is well worth considering (see Chapter 17).

Several provincial governments offer similar savings bonds. They all work along the same lines and they usually offer a somewhat higher rate of interest than the federal government.

One final point to watch: Don't forget about your savings bonds. Once they mature, the interest clock stops ticking. But until you cash them in, the government still has the use of your money. Possibly, you may think the government deserves the break — but it's unlikely. So keep track of the maturity dates of savings bonds that you own and quickly get that money out working for you again. A list of current Canada Savings Bond issues and their maturity dates can be found on page 42. Keep it handy.

CHAPTER 7

On the Deposit Trail

ONCE YOU HAVE SAVED $1,000 or so, you can almost always get a better rate of return by agreeing to lend the money to a financial institution for a fixed period of time instead of keeping it in a savings account, or a money-market mutual fund, where you can get at it any time you want. The institution — bank, trust company or credit union — can afford to pay you a bit more interest when it knows it can hold on to your money for a while. You can take advantage of this by purchasing either a term deposit or a guaranteed investment certificate, and there will be no commission to pay. It's a very competitive business, in fact. The financial pages of daily newspapers are often filled with advertisements offering you what are touted as the best available rates of return on your money. Institutions are constantly thinking up new gimmicks to attract more deposits, which are the lifeblood of their business.

Don't let the hype turn your head and make you forget the fundamentals of the deal you make with the institution. It's a two-way contract. The institution promises you a certain interest rate and you agree to hand over your money for a fixed period of time. This means you are not expected to ask for your money back before the agreed period is over. In many cases, you cannot get your money back at all before the agreed date, no matter how much you need it. In other cases you can, but you will pay a stiff penalty in the form of a big drop in, or perhaps total elimination of, interest payments. You can be pretty sure that you will do worse in that case than if you had left the money in a regular savings account.

There are some technical differences between term deposits, certificates of deposit and guaranteed investment certificates, but they are of little practical consequence to buyers. Indeed, the names used for different kinds of deposits can confuse and mislead you if you are not careful. Whatever the name used, protect yourself by checking out thoroughly the terms and conditions of the deal. Don't be afraid to ask questions and don't let yourself be hurried by financial institutions or made to feel ignorant. They want your money just as much as you want to earn the interest. Make them work for it.

Your first choice will be to decide how long you are willing to let the institution have the use of your money and whether you can be sure you will not need it in the meantime. If you can't be sure you won't need it, you will have to seek out a cashable deposit and probably accept a lower interest rate than you could otherwise get. If you have $1,000 or so to deposit, your choice will usually be limited to one-year to five-year deals. Government deposit insurance covers term deposits and certificates, just like savings accounts. But remember that it does not cover deposits maturing in more than five years (see Chapter 5). Some institutions even accept $500 minimum amounts for deposits of one year or longer. On short-term deposits of less than a year the usual minimum requirement is $5,000. If you have more than $100,000 you will be able to pick your maturity and negotiate the rate individually.

In normal times, the longer you are prepared to tie up your money, the higher the interest rate you will be offered. This is because a longer commitment gives you more chances of being wrong as well as right. If you rent your money out for five years at 8 per cent and interest rates average 10 per cent over the next few years, you are going to feel pretty silly because you will have lost the chance to pick up those extra percentage points of profit. So why not always just take the shortest available term and avoid that risk? You can, but it's also possible for you to rent your money out at 10 per cent for five years while interest rates average 8 per cent over the period. In that case, you will feel pretty smart about doing so much better than other people who were not prepared to take the same risk.

However, hard experience with unpredictable interest rate swings has persuaded many sensible investors not to play the hero with their fixed-income investments. Even though you believe interest rates will certainly be higher a year from now, you don't invest all your capital for a maximum of one year, just in case you are wrong. Similarly, even though you believe interest rates are heading lower, you don't invest all your capital at today's five-year rate, just in case you are wrong (see Chapter 20).

Some of the time there will be little or no difference between the interest rate offered on one-year deposits and on longer-term deposits. And some of the time you will be offered more on a one-year deal than on deals of longer duration. This kind of thing happens when there is a general expectation that interest rates are heading downward and a majority of people want to rent their money out for longer periods to take advantage of today's rates while they last. In order to sell one-year deposits, therefore, the financial institutions have to offer higher rates. It's a demonstration of the law of supply and demand.

Having decided for how long you want to rent your money out, you must then check the available interest rates on offer. You can find out what your own bank or trust company is offering merely by asking. To compare those rates with the general market, however, you will need to cast your eye over the tables of representative deposit rates published regularly in the financial sections of daily newspapers (see Chapter 3). Similar surveys are also available on some electronic information services.

The trickiest aspect of checking available rates is to make sure you are comparing apples with apples, not with oranges. In particular, rates may be quoted with interest paid once a year or twice a year. In the latter case, during the second half of the year you can earn interest on the interest that was earned in the first half of the year — if you don't spend it, that is. With annual payments of interest, you don't have that opportunity. Recall that the more frequently interest is compounded, the higher the effective rate of return. So 10 per cent paid semi-annually and reinvested at the same rate is more than 10 per cent paid annually; it is actually 10.25 per cent. That is why the same institution never offers you as much interest paid semi-annually as interest paid only once a year. Note that the difference gets larger each year because of the continued effect of more frequent compounding. But also note that there is no guarantee you will be able to reinvest the interest at the same rate, unless you have invested in compound-interest certificates where you get the interest only at maturity or when you cash them in. You might be able to get more if interest rates have risen in the meantime, but there's also a chance you will get less.

Maybe you need even more frequent payments of interest, not to reinvest the money but to pay for living expenses. You can arrange for this, too, at some institutions. You can receive your interest quarterly, or even monthly, if you wish. You don't have to buy a 30-day deposit and cash it in each month. The interest you get will be somewhat lower, naturally, than if it were paid every six or 12 months.

You will quickly notice that even after allowing for more frequent compounding, trust companies generally offer higher rates on fixed-term deposits than do the banks. In addition, smaller and lesser-known trust companies pay more than the large household-name trust companies. Stranger still, bank-affiliated mortgage companies offer higher rates than their parent banks do on their regular term deposits. Normally in the financial markets, this kind of difference in interest rates on similar securities reflects the degree of risk you are taking on — the greater the risk, the higher the interest rate. In the case of financial institutions, these differences have persisted even though government deposit insurance more or less equalizes the credit risk between institutions, at least up to the $60,000 limit.

This phenomenon of fixed-term retail-size deposits appears to be mainly a matter of convenience, peace of mind and lack of knowledge. There are many more bank branches across Canada than trust company branches. In downtown areas there often seems to be one on every corner. More people deal with banks for their personal financial services than with trust companies. Most often, they choose which bank to deal with by walking into the most convenient branch and opening an account. If they are generally satisfied with the service and the way the tellers treat them, they usually stay put. They keep their chequing account there, open a savings account from time to time and often put their money into that bank's term deposits or certificates — even if they could get a higher return on their savings with no real additional risk by travelling a few blocks.

It's up to you whether you do things that way. There is no denying that it can be less convenient to deal with a branch of a trust company some distance away. You may have to invest time that you don't feel able or willing to spare. Some people prefer to have a bank's name on their cheques rather than the name of a trust company, especially a small and little-known trust company. This consideration is, of course, irrelevant with term deposits or certificates. But to constantly have to switch money back and forth between different institutions is a bother, too, although it is perfectly practical. You might find, however, that the benefit of the extra interest will be more than offset if you leave money idle for too long in a bank account that doesn't pay interest.

Dealing with small trust companies can also be a problem for your peace of mind. Some companies try to become big too fast and take on too many risks. To win a bigger share of the market, they offer above-average interest rates on deposits. Then, to earn enough to pay the interest, they seek out higher-risk investments that, in turn, pay above-average interest returns. Sometimes, this works and sometimes it doesn't. When it doesn't, the company involved may become the subject of critical media coverage. Worse, it may be forced to merge with a more successful company or even go out of business.

As a retail customer with all your deposits covered by government insurance, your capital will not be at risk even if the company goes bankrupt. You will almost certainly get your money back with whatever interest is due to date within a few weeks.

But there is something called interest risk. Suppose that a week or so before the company collapsed, you had invested in its five-year deposits at an above-average interest rate. Deposit insurance will not cover the interest you would have earned from the date of the bankruptcy until the deposit matures in five years. It covers only interest owing up to the date of the collapse. You face having to reinvest your money at the going rate, which may now be lower.

Having your savings in a collapsing company is a trying experience. As with savings accounts, you may prefer to sacrifice some interest on your fixed-term deposits to avoid these worries.

If you think that putting your money away in term deposits or certificates is more complicated than you believed, professional help is available. Deposit brokers will do all the work for you, most of them free of charge. They survey the market for deposits and advise you about the best deals and the pros and cons of each type of deposit and institution. They also tell you how to stay within the government deposit insurance limits.

In return, you pay them nothing. This unusual deal is possible because some or all of the financial institutions to which the brokers direct the money pay them a commission on the amount deposited. Providing an advice service on deposits also gives the brokers an opportunity to market their other financial advice services for which they do charge fees. You don't have to buy any of the other services; the brokers act strictly as agents. Your money goes directly to the institution, so it is never at risk in the broker's hands. To be sure, write your cheque to the institution.

There might be a possibility of a broker favouring one institution over another at your expense because of differences in the commission paid. It is a very small chance, though. Unlike choosing from different insurance policies or, say, the prospects of different stocks, a deposit broker's customer can easily check the advice given by calling institutions directly or by reading their frequent advertisements. Deposit brokers are usually the source of the tables of deposit rates published in many newspapers. This publicity, too, helps keep the business honest.

CHAPTER 8

Calculating Your Prospects

INVESTING YOUR HARD-EARNED savings is not a charitable enterprise. The idea is not to give money away for nothing — although the way some people go about it, you might think it was. Investments are made in the hope of a tangible return for the risk undertaken, and one of the most important facts for someone considering an investment is how large a return is offered. In simple terms, an investor wants to know how many cents or dollars can be expected on each dollar risked if things work out. The mathematics of calculating this from the information available ranges from very simple arithmetic that many people can perform in their head to complex formulas only a mathematical wizard could handle without the aid of printed tables or electronic devices.

Fortunately, it is not necessary for any investor to do any of these calculations unaided. Today's electronic calculators can handle more than most of us will ever need. A cheap machine doing basic arithmetic is enough for the simpler calculations. Somewhat more expensive calculators designed for investors and financial professionals can supply the answers to the more complicated conundrums. What is important is for investors to understand the meaning of the principal calculations and their results.

The first thing to know is that the return on an investment is more frequently referred to as the yield. Your broker may say that such and such a government bond yields 8 per cent, compared with a 7 per cent return on a five-year certificate of deposit and a 4 per cent yield on a stock. What is he trying to tell you?

In its simplest form, the return, or yield, on any investment is the annual income expressed as a percentage of the cost. Rent $1,000 to your bank by buying a term deposit and you may get $70 in interest a year. That is an annual return, or yield, of 7 per cent, calculated by dividing 70 by 1,000 and multiplying the result by 100. What if you invest the same amount for six months and you get $35 in interest? The yield is still described as 7 per cent — that is, on an equivalent annual basis. If you invest the same amount for six months and actually get $70 in interest, the yield would be a juicy 14 per cent.

The important point to note is that there are always three factors involved in calculating the yield on an investment: the amount invested or at risk, the income received and the period of time for which the investment is made. To make comparisons between different investments possible, however, yields are converted to an equivalent annual basis, whatever the actual period you are dealing with.

Alert readers may already have spotted a problem. The 7 per cent annual yield on the term deposit clearly stays the same throughout the life of the investment, at least so long as you actually get all your $1,000 back, which is usually the case. That is because the market value of the deposit does not vary from day to day. But what about the yield on a stock whose price does vary? When you buy it, the yield is calculated in a similar way to the term deposit example described above. You look up the indicated annual dividend on the stock and figure it out as a percentage of what you paid, ignoring commissions.

Happily, however, the price of the stock may rise the day after. It's been known to happen. Is your yield still the same? In one sense, it is. The size of your original investment has not changed. However, in a more accurate sense, something important has changed. You now have more money at risk than on the previous day. The higher market price of the stock means that you could cash in at a profit. If you choose not to do so, both your original investment and your profit are now at risk. If the dividend has not risen, the real or current yield on each dollar of your investment is less than it was. The reverse is true if the price of the stock falls instead of rising. The real or current yield on your investment is higher than before.

A stock, of course, provides you with no guarantee of getting the full amount of your original investment back. You may get more or you may get less, depending on the market price when you sell. For that reason, only the current yield is taken into account when calculating the income return on a stock. Capital gains may be predicted but they are left as a gleam in an investor's eye, not published routinely as part of the information available.

Instead of a stock or a term deposit, you can invest in a market-able bond sold by a government or a company. Such bonds are like stocks in that their market price varies from hour to hour and day to day throughout their life. They are like term deposits because the seller promises to repay the full face value of your original invest-ment at a fixed date in the future. Yield calculations are further complicated by the fact that although you buy a bond with a face value of $1,000, you may pay more than that for it or you may pay less (see Chapter 10). If you pay the full face value, you are said to have bought the bond at par. Pay more than par and you will be said to have bought at a premium. Pay less than par and you will have bought at a discount.

Clearly, if you pay a premium, you can expect to suffer a capital loss when the bond matures and you get back just the face value. If you buy at a discount, you can expect a nice capital gain when the bond matures and you get the full face value. In each case you can also expect to receive the promised regular interest payments dur-ing the life of the bond, but the return from that income will be ef-fectively shrunk or magnified by the price you paid. This phenomenon is taken into account when investors calculate the yield on marketable bonds. The resulting calculation is known as the yield to maturity, although most of the time you will come across it under the catchall title of "yield." The context should tell you which kind of yield is being talked about, but always check if you are not sure. Note also that to complicate things still more, the quoted prices are based on a fictitious face value of $100 instead of the actual $1,000. So a bond quoted at 98 will actually cost you $980.

It is fairly easy to understand why the yield to maturity on a bond includes both the expected income and the expected capital gain or loss if an investor holds on to the bond until it matures. It is also easy to figure the yield in the rare cases where you buy at par. In fact, the description of a particular bond always includes the promised interest or coupon rate as a percentage of the face value of the bond, which for a purchase at par is the same thing as the yield to maturity.

The details of the calculation of the yield to maturity on a bond bought at a premium or a discount are surprisingly complicated, though. One reason is that the calculation has to take account of when interest payments are made — typically twice a year — and assumes immediate reinvestment of the interest paid. Even professional bond traders hardly ever do the calculation themselves. Indeed, most of them would not know how it is done. Instead, they punch up the price of a bond, its maturity date and its interest rate on some kind of keyboard and electronic circuits do the heavy work. Any broker should be able to supply you with the yield to maturity of a bond you are thinking of buying. If you really want to check it out yourself, the yield to maturity is a standard calculation built into many financial calculators.

The yield to maturity is the only figure to use to compare one bond with another when different maturities and terms are involved. Comparing bonds on the basis of the current yield (interest as a percentage of price) is wholly misleading.

Another problem arises when the terms of a bond allow the issuer to repay or redeem it after a certain date but before it would normally mature. Sometimes redemption will be possible only if a premium is paid. In other cases, the borrower may be able to repay the loan early at par. If a bond is selling in the market at above par when the early redemption date comes around, it is likely that it will be repaid or "called" for redemption. That is because the bond's premium price means the interest rate required to sell that type of bond has gone down since it was originally issued (see Chapter 10). The issuer will, therefore, probably find it pays to repay it and replace it with new bonds paying less interest. If, on the other hand, a bond is selling at a discount, it is unlikely to be redeemed early because replacing it with new bonds would require payment of a higher interest rate.

The rule for calculating the yield to maturity is:
• For bonds selling at a premium, use the earliest redemption date (often called the call date) in the calculation instead of the scheduled maturity date. The result is that the capital loss absorbed each year will be larger.
• For bonds selling at a discount or below the call price, use the scheduled maturity date. That way, the capital gain recognized each year will be smaller than if the earliest call date were used.

Things get even more complicated with so-called serial issues. These are bonds typically issued by municipal governments that mature over a number of years rather than all at once. Part of the original amount is repaid in year one, more in year two and so on.

You must use weighted averages to figure the yield to maturity on these bonds, and that is best left to the experts.

So far in this chapter, all yield calculations have ignored income tax. Where a profit or loss results from interest payments only, calculation of the after-tax yield is reasonably straightforward and follows the normal rules for investment income (see Chapter 18). As we have seen, though, bonds bought at a discount produce capital gains when they mature and bonds bought at a premium produce capital losses. Therefore, the capital gains tax rules come into play. Given an investor's assumed tax rate, it is possible to calculate the after-tax yield to maturity on a particular bond bought at a certain price. Again, however, it is a complicated business best left to electronic calculators and those who know how to use them.

Investing in mortgages is a form of fixed-income investing (see Chapter 15). In the typical arrangement, you lend money toward the cost of a house or other real estate. The loan is repaid or amortized over an agreed period through regular fixed payments, usually once a month, that include a portion of the principal as well as the interest due. At the start, most of the payment is interest. As the amount owing is reduced, the interest portion shrinks and the amount of principal repaid increases. Eventually all the principal is paid off and there is no more interest to pay. Believe me, it works out, although perhaps not in your lifetime if you are the borrower.

The calculation of the fixed payments is done in a way that produces the agreed interest return on the amount of money still owing each month. It is a type known technically as an ordinary annuity calculation. Again, many financial calculators have the calculation built in and so do most computer spreadsheet programs. All you have to do is enter the amount being borrowed, the interest rate and the period over which the loan is to be paid off.

However, there is a source of major confusion for Canadians because our law requires the interest to be handled differently from the normal method used for mortgages in the U.S. and from the method used generally in both countries for other loans. Payments on most loans are made monthly and interest is also calculated monthly. Mortgage payments are treated similarly in the U.S., but in Canada interest can be compounded only semi-annually — that is, twice a year instead of 12 times a year. As a result, the monthly payment required to pay off or amortize a Canadian mortgage loan is a little lower than a U.S. mortgage loan at the same interest rate.

Calculating Mortgage Payments Canadian-Style

Monthly payments on a Canadian mortgage are lower than on a comparable U.S. mortgage because interest is paid only semi-annually and not in advance. The easy way to calculate them is with a computer spreadsheet, most of which have a function that requires you merely to supply figures for the amount borrowed, the term over which it is to be paid off and the interest rate. However, such spreadsheets usually use the U.S. method. To get the Canadian figure, you have to substitute the following formula for the interest-rate entry:

$$\left(\frac{annual\ rate}{2} + 1\right)^{\frac{1}{6}} - 1$$

The hard way is to use the following formulas, either in a spreadsheet or with an electronic calculator.

1. With r the annual interest rate, first calculate monthly interest rate (i) this way:

$$i = (1 + 0.5r)^{\frac{1}{6}} - 1$$

2. Then use it in the following formula for the monthly payment, where P is the amount borrowed, N the number of months and M the constant payment:

$$M = \frac{P \times i}{1 - (1 + i)^{-N}}$$

TABLE IX

The difference appears negligible for small amounts but it adds up to a sizable figure on today's large and costly mortgages. For example, the monthly payment on a $100,000 mortgage at 9 per cent over 25 years would be $839.20, calculated U.S.-style. On a similar Canadian mortgage the monthly payment would be $827.98. A formula for adjusting the interest rate on Canadian mortgages that you can plug into a spreadsheet such as Lotus 123, Microsoft Excel or Borland Quattro is shown in Table IX.

One other kind of return-on-investment calculation is worth mentioning, even though few fixed-income investors will ever need it. The internal rate of return calculation, or IRR, is designed to handle situations where there is a cash return over a period of time but in differing amounts and perhaps not in every period. A typical ex-

Selected Present Values of $1.00

AT VARIOUS INTEREST RATES (IN CENTS)

End of year	10%	11%	12%	13%	14%	15%
1	90.91	90.09	89.29	88.50	87.72	86.96
2	82.64	81.16	79.72	78.31	76.95	75.61
3	75.13	73.12	71.18	69.31	67.50	65.75
4	68.30	65.87	63.55	61.33	59.21	57.18
5	62.09	59.35	56.74	54.28	51.94	49.72
6	56.45	53.46	50.66	48.03	45.56	43.23
7	51.32	48.17	45.23	42.51	39.96	37.59
8	46.65	43.39	40.39	37.62	35.06	32.69
9	42.41	39.09	36.06	33.29	30.75	28.43
10	38.55	35.22	32.20	29.46	26.97	24.72
11	35.05	31.73	28.75	26.07	23.66	21.49
12	31.86	28.58	25.67	23.07	20.76	18.69
13	28.97	25.75	22.92	20.42	18.21	16.25
14	26.33	23.20	20.46	18.07	15.97	14.13
15	23.94	20.90	18.27	15.99	14.01	12.29
16	21.76	18.83	16.31	14.15	12.29	10.69
17	19.78	16.96	14.56	12.52	10.78	9.29
18	17.99	15.28	13.00	11.08	9.46	8.08
19	16.35	13.77	11.61	9.81	8.29	7.03
20	14.86	12.40	10.37	8.68	7.28	6.11

TABLE X

ample would be an investment where there was no return, or where there were losses, in the early years — known euphemistically as negative cash flows. Another example would be a stock that paid no dividends when you bought it but later started to pay some. Annuity calculations cannot handle this sort of thing because they are based on unchanging payments in each period. IRR calculations are not something to be tackled casually, however. They are best handled by specialist financial calculators and computer spreadsheet programs, and even then you need to pay close attention to what you are doing to produce meaningful results.

A key idea behind this calculation is a concept called the net present value of an investment. As you become a more proficient investor, it is vital for you to understand clearly that a dollar you receive in the future is worth less than a dollar you have in your hand today. There are two reasons for this. First, it is one of the safest bets in history that inflation is going to continue and that your future dollar will buy less than today's dollar. Second, if you have a dollar today and you just put it in the bank, you can earn some interest on it. You won't be able to do that with your future dollar until you get it.

Is there a way to figure out how much less your future dollar is worth? To put it another way, what is the real value today of your future dollar? Present-value calculations provide an answer. They are based on a simple principle: The value of your future dollar depends on the interest rate you choose for your particular calculation. For example, using an annual interest rate of 10 per cent, $1 due at the end of five years has a value today of 62.09 cents (see Table X). This reflects the fact that if you invest 62 cents today at 10 per cent interest and leave the money alone for five years, you will have $1. If you use an interest rate of 14 per cent instead, the value today of a dollar you will receive in five years' time is just under 52o cents. Using 6 per cent, the present value of the dollar is almost 75 cents.

Obviously, present values vary widely with different interest-rate assumptions, so how do you use this technique to evaluate a proposed investment? There are several steps. First, you must choose the minimum after-tax rate of return you are prepared to accept on the investment. To do that, your starting point is the rate of return available on other kinds of investment, in particular on those with very little risk. You might choose 10 per cent if that was the going rate on term deposits or guaranteed investment certificates, which would leave you with 6 per cent after tax if your marginal tax rate is 40 per cent. Then you assess the degree of risk in the sort of investment you are evaluating, relative to the deposit. If it is no riskier, you can set your required rate of return at 6 per cent after tax, too. If you judge that it is twice as risky, you should double your required return to 12 per cent after tax or 20 per cent before tax.

What you are doing here is saying to yourself: If I can get 6 per cent after tax with virtually no risk, I need the prospect of a whole lot more than that to go into something that's much riskier. It is merely a systematic process of applying common sense to deciding whether to make an investment. Consciously, or more often unconsciously, every investor goes through the same process when making an investment.

Once you have chosen your required return, the next step is to list all the expected net after-tax cash returns each year from the investment. Then you calculate the present value of each year's return by using the required rate of return you have chosen. It is this step that gives the technique its generic name: discounted cash flow analysis. Total the answers and the result is the net present value of the investment. If it is a negative number, that is a warning sign that you should perhaps steer clear of this particular golden opportunity. If it is close to zero, the investment should perform more or less in line with your expectations — if you made the right choice, that is. If the net present value is positive, the investment should perform better than your expectations, again subject to getting the predicted cash flows reasonably accurate.

Note that there is a vitally important assumption built into net present value calculations. This is the assumption that you can reinvest all the cash returns on your investment during its life at your required rate of return. This may be unrealistic, especially if the proposed investment is so risky that you have rightly chosen an unusually high rate of required return.

CHAPTER 9

Do You Need a Broker?

YOU DON'T HAVE TO DEAL with a broker to rent your money out. In fact, you can spend a lifetime earning interest from lending your savings and never go near a broker. To some investors who have had unhappy experiences with brokers, this may be one of the attractions of fixed-income investing. For others who do find a good broker and make money from lending their money as well as investing it in stocks, the partnership can be very rewarding.

Brokers are not, however, set up to compete effectively with your local branch of a bank, trust company or credit union for small amounts of money committed to earn interest. They aren't encouraged by their employers to sell a few thousand dollars of guaranteed investment certificates. They will perform this service for clients who bring other more rewarding business their way, but brokers can't make a living doing that sort of business all the time. They will also sell you all the fixed-income investments described in this book, but they will be much happier if the amounts involved are much larger than your typical stock-market transaction. That's because brokers, like all other sales representatives, live or die on the commissions or fees they make from their clients. Unless you give them some business, they earn nothing.

If you start doing some of your fixed-income investing through a broker, you may initially be confused by the absence of any mention of a commission. You will be quoted an interest rate and hand over your money. But there is always the equivalent of a commission paid somewhere and built into the transaction. Most fixed-income investments handled by brokers involve the firm buying the merchandise at one price and selling it at a marked-up price.

There's nothing extraordinary about this, of course. All business rests on the same principle, and the markups in the financial industry can be considered small compared with those in some other businesses. It's also true that commissions get smaller with bigger volume. The markup on $100,000 worth of government bonds will be smaller than on $10,000. There is also a markup built into the purchase price of stocks, although it's not so visible. On top of that, you are charged a specific commission by the broker. In fixed-income investing, it's all handled with a single markup, usually a maximum of 1 per cent.

One of the most common complaints of customers who buy and sell bonds through their brokers is that the price they pay is more than the price they see quoted on the financial pages of newspapers, or the price they receive when selling is less than the quoted price. Customers often feel they are getting ripped off, although that's not normally the case. The published prices are, in a sense, wholesale or supplier prices, usually on transactions of a million dollars or more.

Should you bother with a broker at all? Probably not, if your fixed-income investing is restricted to savings bonds, term deposits or guaranteed investment certificates and you are never going to venture into the stock market. A broker is unlikely to earn enough from catering to those limited fixed-income needs to make it worthwhile to pay sufficient attention to your investments. If your fixed-income investing extends to bonds, treasury bills, money-market funds and the like, a good broker can be very useful. He or she can give you useful advice on your overall investment activities. In the best of cases, you will have a personal financial adviser rather than a mere seller of bonds or stocks.

Word-of-mouth recommendations are the best way to find a good broker. Get recommendations from friends or relatives. Don't just go by the reputation and size of the firm; brokers are more like independent contractors than employees. A big, established firm probably ensures reasonable standards of honesty and competency, but don't count on it — especially at times when a roaring bull market in stocks has brought in a flood of inexperienced newcomers. Good brokers can be found at big and small firms, at firms that have been around forever and firms that opened their doors just last month.

Don't be reluctant to go through a period of trial and error in search of a good broker. Dealing with your money is a very personal and often emotional thing. The broker your best friend swears by may drive you around the bend. There are different styles for different folks, so if you're unhappy, don't tough it out. A marriage is worth working at for a long time, but not a relationship with a broker. Just pay what you owe, say polite goodbyes and move on. However, when you find a good broker you feel comfortable with and who helps you make smart decisions about your money, hang on tight. Frequently, if such a paragon moves on to another firm, it will be worthwhile for you to move your business to the new firm.

A broker with whom you start doing business will have questions to ask you, too. There is, for a start, some personal information required by stock exchange and government regulations. Your broker will want your name, address, telephone number and social insurance number (required by the tax laws). In addition, you will be asked how much you know about investing, how much income you have, what assets you own and how much you owe. You will also be asked about your investment objectives. "To make a lot of money in a hurry" will not be a sufficient answer. One crucial question is whether you plan safety-first investing or are interested in taking more risks in search of bigger profits.

You may consider these questions impertinent, but there are reasons for them. Reason one is a benefit to you. A good broker will use the knowledge to steer you toward investments you understand and which are suitable to your financial state.

Reason two is a benefit to your broker, who naturally wants to get paid for his or her work. The practices of the investment business mean that brokers take considerable credit risks with their clients. There are few other businesses in which such large amounts of money are committed on nothing more than a telephone conversation, a fax or a message on a computer terminal. If you tell your broker on the phone to buy $100,000 worth of bonds for you, the firm may already have those bonds in inventory. Frequently, though, the firm will go out and buy them from another firm to sell to you. Both transactions will be settled several days later. In the meantime, with financial markets as excitable as they are these days, the market price of the bonds may drop sharply. When you come to pay for your purchase, you may already be a loser. You, of course, would not be tempted to back out of the deal. But it does happen now and then, as brokers well know. The rules of the game frequently put the broker on the hook for any losses caused by a customer's failure to pay.

So when you are answering all those questions about your personal finances, your prospective broker is also trying to decide whether you are going to turn into a deadbeat. If the broker is suspicious, the firm may call for a credit check, just like your friendly loan officer at the bank.

After you've been dealing with a broker for a while, how do you go about assessing whether you've found a good one? Here are some questions to ask yourself:

What is your broker's batting average? In other words, is the advice you get pretty good? You can't expect a 100 per cent record, but over a period of time, allowing for all the circumstances including your own pigheadedness, is the relationship profitable to you?

Do you get the feeling your broker never listens to you? Is your broker the kind who calls you indiscriminately to push whatever the firm wants pushed? Are the investment ideas from your broker based on accurate information and well thought out? Do they make sense to you more often than not?

Do the two of you get along personally, or do you always feel vaguely irritated or unhappy after you have a chat? The personal chemistry is important and life is too short to put up with the wrong mix when you don't have to.

Too many negative answers to such questions should make you consider a change. Remember, however, that you may be a cause of the problem. In business relationships just as much as in personal relationships, mutual respect and politeness usually produce the best results.

Occasionally, you may come across a broker who behaves dishonestly or ignores your instructions. You don't have to put up with such behaviour. There are strict rules of conduct for brokers, backed up by legal penalties, and few firms relish the bad publicity an angry client can produce. Your first step is to complain to the broker's branch manager. If you get nowhere with the firm, you can take your complaint to the local office of the brokerage industry's trade group, the Investment Dealers Association of Canada, or to the stock exchange where a questionable transaction took place or where the firm is a member. As a last resort, you can go to provincial government securities regulators.

These bodies all have considerable legal powers to investigate and punish brokers within their jurisdiction. At this serious stage, remember to put everything in writing.

CHAPTER 10

Bond Market Basics

MONEY IS RENTED OUT IN HUGE quantities every day by investors who buy bonds sold by governments and corporations. Just as when you buy a term deposit or a guaranteed investment certificate, buying a bond means that you become a creditor of the original issuer. The piece of paper you may get is a promise to repay borrowed money on a particular date and in the meantime to pay interest. Like a dollar bill, it is elaborately designed and printed to make forgery difficult and carries an identification number and the signature or signatures of the signing officers of the body that issued it. Sometimes, interest coupons are attached. You remove these as they fall due and turn them in to be cashed at a financial institution. Other bonds do not have attached coupons, with the interest paid instead by cheque to the registered owner. Still others exist only as entries in an electronic bookkeeping system. Guard any paper coupons and bonds as you would dollar bills because whoever has possession of them is presumed to be the owner. Don't keep them in a cupboard at home — use a safety deposit box or put them in safekeeping with your broker.

You have already become familiar with one broad category of government bonds: savings bonds (see Chapter 6). Recall that you could turn those in for cash but you could not sell them to anybody else. Governments, together with corporations, sell another category of bonds that can be bought and sold like stocks. They are called marketable bonds and there are many billions of dollars' worth of them outstanding. Confusingly, you will sometimes see these bonds referred to as debentures. The technical difference is that a bond issuer's promise to repay the borrowed money is backed up by the pledge of certain assets as security. In contrast, a debenture is an unsecured promise to repay the money. However, the term "bond" is often used interchangeably to refer to bonds and debentures.

Bonds are a classic form of fixed-income investment. The original buyer lends money to the issuer for a period of time in return for a promise of regular, and usually fixed, interest payments. So long as they do not affect the issuer's ability to pay the promised interest and eventually repay the borrowed money, the financial fortunes of the borrower are irrelevant to the investor. A corporation that has issued bonds may perhaps double or triple its profits and therefore double or triple the dividends paid on its stock. The owners of its bonds will still get exactly what they were promised — no more and no less. A government that has issued bonds can, and frequently does, run its operations at a huge annual deficit, but the owners of its bonds still receive regular interest payments and eventually get their money back.

There is an added kicker to owning marketable bonds, however. Before they mature you may be able to sell them in the bond market at a higher price than you paid for them and take a pleasant capital gain in addition to any interest payments you have received. Incidentally, when you sell a bond, the buyer pays you any accrued but unpaid interest in addition to the market price. If your sale occurs 20 days after the last interest payment, for instance, the buyer is on the hook for the interest you earned for those 20 days but which he will eventually receive on the next interest payment date. Alternatively, if you need or just want most of your money back before a bond matures, you can choose to sell your bond in that same market and accept a lower price than you paid for it. In other words, like stocks, the market prices of bonds go up and down.

Why marketable bond prices vary from day to day is not immediately obvious — unlike stocks, where changing assessments of a company's business fortunes provide an easily understandable reason. Let's look a little more closely to understand what's going on. The key is that the interest rate on a bond is almost always fixed at the time of its issue.

Suppose you buy a $1,000 marketable government bond maturing in 10 years at a time when such bonds pay interest of 10 per cent. A year later the going interest rate on similar new bonds has fallen to 8 per cent. Would you sell your 10 per cent bond to somebody else at the same price you paid for it? Not unless you were not paying attention. However, there is a price at which you probably would sell, but it has to be higher than you paid. How much higher? Recall that, when other factors such as the income remain the same, the yield on an investment goes down as the price rises. Mathematically, there is a premium price at which the yield to maturity for your 10 per cent bond falls to approximately 8 per cent. Somewhere around that price, there will frequently be a buyer willing to pay up and a seller — you — willing to cash out at a profit.

Now suppose the reverse has happened. The interest rate required to sell bonds similar to your one-year-old 10 per cent bond has risen to 12 per cent. No one in their right mind is going to pay you the full amount that you paid for your bond at a time when similar new bonds can be had at a price that provides a return two percentage points higher. So if you want to sell, you will have to cut your price to raise the yield. By how much? Again, there is a discount price at which the yield to maturity on your 10 per cent bond rises to a competitive 12 per cent or so. Probably you will find a buyer somewhere around that price.

The rule is:
- Interest rates up, bond prices down;
- Interest rates down, bond prices up.

Think of it as a playground seesaw, with interest rates at one end and bond prices at the other.

Note that none of this has anything to do with changes in the bond issuer's financial condition and prospects. Yields do vary from issuer to issuer, depending on the credit standing and financial circumstances of the borrower, and do change from time to time as those characteristics change. However, most price changes in the bond market most of the time reflect actual and expected changes in interest rates in general.

Finding out the market price of bonds you own is not quite as simple a task as checking the price of your stocks. That is because almost all bonds are bought and sold in a very different manner. There is no stock exchange floor and no easily accessible stock ticker publishing a minute-to-minute record of transactions. Bonds change hands over a vast telecommunications network between traders buying and selling as owners or principals, not as agents as they do with stocks. Place an order with your broker and she will sell you some bonds from her firm's holdings, or the firm's trader will buy the bonds from somebody else and resell them to you. At each stage of the process the buyer becomes the actual owner of the bonds, if only for a moment or two. The minor exception is an order for the handful of bond issues that are listed on stock exchanges.

At the centre of this network in Canada are a handful of specialist brokers who act as intermediaries between bond dealers and banks. They maintain a system of video screens that provide traders at the dealers and banks with up-to-date information about available bonds and their market price quotations. The major advantage they offer is anonymity. If a dealer's trader has some bonds for sale, he posts the offering on the system at his asking price. Other participants in the system can see the offering and respond with a bid but they do not know who the seller is until a deal is actually made. The operations of these specialist brokers are regulated by the industry's trade group, the Investment Dealers Association of Canada, under the overall supervision of government securities regulators. Unlike most bond market participants, they operate strictly as agents and are paid commissions for their services.

Representative lists of bond quotations are published in daily and weekly newspapers. Check them out and you will see major differences between them and the stock exchange quotations. For each bond there is the name of the issuer in shorthand form: for example, Canada, for the federal government. This is followed by the coupon or interest rate and the maturity date, also in shorthand form. You will often hear particular bond issues identified by these key facts. For example, your broker may refer in conversation to the "Canada 6-and-a-halfs of '04," meaning 6.5 per cent bonds issued by the federal government and maturing in 2004. Those particular bonds mature in June and other Canada bonds mature in other months of the same year. Ottawa has had to sell a lot of bonds to cover its annual deficits. It is rarely necessary, however, to spell out a particular month so long as there is no other issue maturing in the same year with the same interest rate.

In some tables this shorthand description is followed by a single price. In other tables, you will see a column of bid prices and a second column of always-higher ask prices. Then there is a column for the yield and often a column giving either the change in price or yield from the previous listing. One major item of information missing is the volume of transactions. Because transactions in the bond market are not reported and recorded in one place, this information is not available. For the same reason there is no report of the highest and lowest prices paid during the trading session.

You should be aware that any single price quoted in these lists is only an approximation of the last price of the session. It is often the midpoint between the final bid and ask quotations. If you ask your broker to quote you a price on a bond he will give you either the bid price or the ask, or offered, price. The bid price is what you get if you are selling bonds. The ask price is what you pay if you are buying bonds. Naturally, the bid price is lower than the ask. You should also be aware that unless you are dealing in million-dollar amounts or more, you will usually pay more to buy bonds than the published quotation, and get less from selling bonds. Don't abuse your broker when you discover this; it's built into the system.

The practice of quoting bid and ask prices is so fundamental to the bond market, and to other financial markets, that it is crucial for you to understand clearly how it works. Bid and ask quotations are at the heart even of the stock market, although you will often not be aware of it when you buy or sell stocks. People who have bought a car or a house are familiar with the idea even though different language is used. As a buyer, you offer a bid price you figure you can afford to pay, or can get away with. The seller quotes you a higher asking price that he says is the minimum he is willing to accept. Depending on the state of the market in cars or houses, and often on the relative bargaining skills of the buyer or the seller, any transaction will actually be closed somewhere within the range established by the bid and ask prices. Frequently, no deal will be done because no acceptable compromise is reached.

It's the same with stocks and bonds. Professional traders spend their working lives quoting bid and ask prices and making deals within those limits. Then they turn around and quote a bid and ask price to somebody else. Traders live on the difference between the price they paid for the securities and the price for which they sell them to somebody else. This difference is called the price spread, or the spread for short. Sometimes you will hear it called the markup. It should not be confused, however, with the yield or interest spread between two different bonds that we will encounter later.

Like any other business, there is a volume discount. It costs more or less the same to handle a $10-million order as a $10,000 order. So the spread or markup on the former is always a lot smaller than the latter. This is true of stocks as well as bonds, but when you buy a stock you usually pay a commission to your broker on top of the price. In contrast, with bonds, you do not pay a separate commission. You pay a price that is marked up to provide the seller with a profit instead. Similarly, if you are selling bonds, the price you get

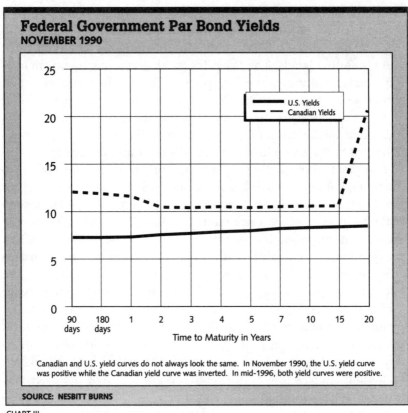

Federal Government Par Bond Yields
NOVEMBER 1990

Legend: U.S. Yields / Canadian Yields

Time to Maturity in Years

Canadian and U.S. yield curves do not always look the same. In November 1990, the U.S. yield curve was positive while the Canadian yield curve was inverted. In mid-1996, both yield curves were positive.

SOURCE: NESBITT BURNS

CHART III

is marked down to provide the buyer with the equivalent of a commission. In effect, the commission is built into the price.

This system makes it difficult for an individual customer to know the true price of a bond. Frequently on small orders for individuals, the sales representative you deal with is taking a commission of up to one point on the transaction by his firm. You may pay, say, 98 for bonds that were "transferre" by the firm to the sales representative for 97. Remember that these shorthand quotations actually refer to bonds with a face value of $1,000. Your price is $980 for each bond. The sales representative's cut varies with the size of the order, how much trading the customer does and whether the particular bonds are actively traded in the market. On small orders below $10,000, a minimum dollar charge may come into effect.

What the firm's bond department paid for your bonds in the first place is a business secret, however. The bonds may have cost 96, in which case the firm makes a handsome profit, or they may have cost 99, in which case the firm is accepting a loss. Why would any firm do that? It may be because its traders expect interest rates to rise and therefore bond prices to fall. So they decide to take a small loss today to avoid having to take a bigger loss tomorrow.

That might seem to make you the fool for buying bonds today that will be worth less tomorrow and would have been available more cheaply then. It's possible, however, that the firm's traders are wrong about interest rates. It has been known to happen. Perhaps this very day rates are about to start falling and the market value of your bonds will start rising. Like the stock market, the bond market offers even small players the chance to be profitably right at the expense of big-time players who call the shots wrongly. It's not easy but it can be done.

Opportunities also exist for dedicated bond market players who take the trouble to learn about the so-called yield curve. You would expect that money borrowed for long periods would carry a higher interest rate than money borrowed for short periods, and for much of the time that is so. One reason is that inflation takes a bigger toll on the eventual repayment after 20 years than after three years. Another is that 20 years gives much more opportunity for things to go wrong. However, the relationship between the actual yields on short-term bonds and on long-term bonds changes a great deal.

Bond market professionals track this relationship by plotting on a graph the yields for bonds of a similar category of issuer but with different terms to maturity. This might be done, for example, for federal government bonds ranging from 90 days to 20 years (see example in Chart III). When this is done in varying market conditions over a period of time, you find that the shape and slope of the line joining the plotted yields at any particular time changes. Sometimes, there is a big difference between short-term yields and higher long-term yields, so the line slopes upward steeply. At other times, there is hardly any difference, so the line is more or less flat.

Every now and then, yields on short-term bonds may move considerably above the yields on similar longer-term bonds. The resulting line on the graph is known as an inverted yield curve. Typically, this occurs when borrowers have a strong appetite for money but interest rates are expected to fall in the near future. In those circumstances, the borrowers need to attract lenders but are reluctant to make commitments for long periods at today's high interest rates. Conversely, lenders or buyers of bonds would prefer longer-term commitments at today's rates. To lure them into short-term deals therefore requires borrowers to pay higher rates.

Within a diversified portfolio of bonds there are many ways to take profitable advantage of the changing yield curve. For example, if you believe interest rates are heading lower, you might find it possible to extend the term of your investment and lock in today's rate by switching from a bond with an early maturity date to another bond of similar quality but maturing several years later. Because of momentary market anomalies, this can sometimes be done by selling and buying at almost the same price.

It is also worth noting that when interest rates rise, the prices of longer-term bonds fall further and faster than the prices of shorter-term bonds. The reverse is also true: Falling interest rates produce a bigger increase in long-term bond prices than in the prices of short-term bonds. In addition, the prices of bonds with lower interest coupons usually change more than those of high-coupon bonds. These phenomena suggest that you can take advantage of interest rate swings by well-timed bond switches. You shorten the average term of your portfolio and buy more high-coupon bonds when rates start to rise. You lengthen the average term and buy more low-coupon bonds when rates start to fall.

Success in this tricky business will provide a bigger return than the average coupon income you would get from leaving your bond portfolio undisturbed. It is, however, a game mainly for professionals. It requires close intimacy with the market and considerable capital with which to buy enough bonds to make the acquisition costs reasonable. Above all, it demands the ability to call changes in interest rate trends early and accurately, something that most mere mortals find extremely difficult. Amateurs should avoid it unless they are prepared to put in enough time to learn the strategy and tactics and to pay close enough attention to the state of play.

CHAPTER 11

Getting Your Money Back

ON THE FACE OF IT, LENDING money to a government that uses most of it to pay interest on previously borrowed money does not sound like a good idea. Few people would lend money to an individual in the same straits. Yet the federal government, which does exactly that with the billions of dollars it borrows each year, has the highest credit rating of all Canadian bond issuers. And the credit ratings of provincial governments, most of which also borrow large amounts to cover the gap between what they spend each year and what they raise in taxes, are not much lower. Why? It's because these governments have legally unlimited powers to raise revenue through taxes. Unlike companies, whose ability to pay interest on bonds they sell and repay the borrowed money when due depends on taking in enough cash from customers who can usually go elsewhere if they wish, governments can compel their taxpayers to supply the money to meet their obligations. In addition, the federal government has the power to create money through the operations of the government-owned Bank of Canada and the commercial banking system.

For these reasons and because most people find it unthinkable that the national government could go bankrupt, the system of assessing the ability of bond issuers to pay the promised interest and otherwise meet their obligations as they fall due is anchored by the top rating given to the debt of the federal government. Ratings of other bond issuers — provincial and municipal governments, corporations and other bodies — are scaled down from that level and interest rates required on their bonds are scaled upward from the rates on federal bonds.

Few bond investors have the time or the inclination to do the analysis needed to assign credit ratings to government and corporate borrowers. The market depends heavily on the services of analysts who specialize in this line of work. In Canada, two firms dominate the business: Dominion Bond Rating Service in Toronto and Canadian Bond Rating Service in Montreal. They provide independent and objective assessments against which to check the sometimes overenthusiastic judgments of the people involved in selling a bond issue to investors. To maintain their independence they do not manage money for investors, nor buy and sell securities, nor recommend securities for purchase or sale. Their customers are professionals who invest large amounts of other people's money, such as pension fund and portfolio managers at banks, trust companies and other large financial institutions. Many such money managers do their own credit analysis and use the rating firms' conclusions to cross-check their own. Two well-known rating firms in the U.S. are Moody's Investors Service and Standard & Poor's.

The two Canadian firms rate the federal government's issues and the debt of other provinces, municipalities and corporations. When a new issue of bonds is launched, the firms issue an initial credit rating. They review these ratings as circumstances change. Individual bond investors will rarely find it necessary to subscribe to these services directly. Almost as soon as they are issued, the ratings become common knowledge throughout the investment community. Your broker should always be able to supply you with an up-to-date rating on any bond in which you are interested.

The higher the credit rating the less interest the borrower has to pay on its bonds. There are minor differences in the terminology used by the firms, but their rating scales all range from the highest quality triple-A classification down to extremely risky C-grade categories (see example in Table XI). The ratings are essentially indicators designed to help answer the single most crucial question for all bond investors: If I lend my money to this particular borrower, how probable is it that I will get it back at the agreed time and in the meantime receive uninterrupted payments of interest? The highest promised return in history means little if the answer to this question is "not very probable at all."

The ratings are relative, not absolute. They are assessments of the credit risk of one borrower in relation to others. Because of overall conditions, all borrowers may be higher risks at one point in time than at another, during a sharp economic downturn, for example. Their relative positions may not have changed, however.

You might see the top quality triple-A rating written as AAA, A++ or even A**. It indicates that if you don't get all the principal

Bond Rating Classifications

Rating	Description
AAA	Near perfection
AA	Well above average
A	Upper medium grade
BBB	Medium grade
BB	Mildly speculative
B	Middle speculative
CCC	Highly speculative
CC	In default
C	Second tier of debt of company in default

SOURCE: DOMINION BOND RATING SERVICE

TABLE XI

and interest you were promised, this will come as a total surprise to everybody. As one rating service puts it more formally, "The degree of protection afforded principal and interest is of the highest order."

Applied to a government, it indicates that the borrower's ability to levy taxes to meet obligations is not threatened by economic decline or by an exodus of highly productive people. The government's financial management is reasonably well regarded and it is not so heavily in debt in relation to the size of the economy on which it can draw for tax revenue as to put in doubt its ability to pay. Applied to a company, the rating means that the firm's profits are stable or increasing steadily. The industry or industries in which it operates are also stable, not in decline. There is also no reason to suspect that any of this will change in the foreseeable future. Finally, the size of the company's cash flow and the financial strength of its balance sheet make the possibility that its cheques will bounce seem remote.

The double-A rating, written sometimes as AA, A+ or A*, reflects just the tiniest doubt about any or all of the above factors. The investment quality of the governments or companies with this rating is still very high and there is almost 100 per cent certainty that all the interest and principal will be paid when due. Double-A-rated borrowers are like a prosperous family about whose financial strength the neighbours are just starting to speculate. In short, it is one notch down from the highest category.

With the single-A rating, you drop to a whole new classification: medium grade. Bonds with this rating are in the upper tier of this second-level classification and they are still good quality investments. It will still come as a surprise if the governments and companies concerned fail to pay every dollar they owe when due, plus the promised interest. However, the protection of interest and principal they offer is not quite of the same order and they may be more vulnerable to bad economic times.

Bonds with a triple-B rating are in the middle of the medium-grade classification. You may see this rating written as BBB, B++ or perhaps B**. Your interest and principal have merely adequate protection but the borrower is considered quite vulnerable to worsening economic times. There may also be other special factors in this borrower's financial situation to worry about.

Within each rating category you may see subdivisions, such as AA (Low) or A (High). The triple-B rating is the bottom of the scale for many institutional investors. They don't bother looking at anything with a lower rating, and that's not a bad policy for individual investors to follow as well. Renting your money out for a fixed return works best when you get all the interest you were promised and you get all your capital back. The returns available in the fixed-income market are not usually good enough to compensate for high-risk ventures.

For those interested in taking on more risk in search of above-average returns, there are even lower ratings. The double-B classification is in the bottom tier of the medium-grade category. It indicates the bonds are mildly speculative. There is some risk of not getting all your interest paid and all your capital returned, especially in bad economic times. This may be because the company is fairly small and does not have the financial strength to ride through business reverses unscathed. Single-B bonds are just plain speculative. Buy them and you will face a serious risk of not receiving interest or not having your capital repaid.

With a triple-C rating, you enter the world of highly speculative investments where there is a clear and present danger of default on interest and principal. A double-C rating means that the default has already happened and the only question is how much is available to satisfy financial obligations to creditors. The single-C rating is the lowest of the low and it indicates that the chance of getting anything back is remote.

Rating government borrowers is a technical and problematic exercise probably best left to the professional experts. For all practical purposes, an individual investor can make the assumption that lending money to the federal government involves little risk of not getting paid back with interest. For one thing, since the federal government is the ultimate lender of last resort to the entire financial system, we would all have much more to worry about than getting paid interest on its bonds if there were signs that it was about to go bankrupt. Decisions on whether to buy particular provincial and municipal bonds should also be guided by experts' judgments.

Do-it-yourself analysis of the credit risk of a particular corporate bond or debenture is a more practical proposition for an individual investor. You can still choose to rely on the professionals' ratings, but you can also decide to make some of the tests yourself. At the very least, this should enable you to understand what your broker is talking about when he recommends a particular issue.

The first and most important test is known as interest coverage. Interest payments are tax-deductible, so a company pays the interest on its bonds out of what's left after paying all operating expenses except income taxes. Common sense suggests that there should be enough money available each year to meet that obligation with a comfortable margin of safety. The bigger that margin, the higher the investment quality of the bonds. It is true, of course, that a company may soldier on year after year with little or no margin of safety and meet all its financial obligations. The risk that one year it will fail to do so is high, however, and that should always be reflected in the credit rating of its bonds or debentures.

To calculate the interest coverage, you first add up the earnings available to make interest payments. Get hold of the company's most recent annual report, skim over the pictures and the inspiring words from the management and dig out the income statement from the financial statistics. Look for the line that reports the net profit after tax but before any extraordinary items. Add back to it any minority interest you see reported on the income statement, plus all income taxes and the actual interest charges for its most recently available accounting years. Then divide this amount by the interest charges. The process should be repeated for the most recent five years to get a clear picture of a company's financial performance over time. Many companies helpfully provide a five-year historical summary of key numbers from their financial statements in their annual reports and some even calculate the interest coverage for you. Your broker should be willing to help if you get stuck.

Rule-of-thumb minimum standards provide a starting point for assessing the results of these calculations. Utilities such as telephone companies or natural gas distributors typically have many bond issues and large annual interest bills. However, their earnings do not generally fluctuate as much as industrial companies. So interest coverage of at least two times in each year is usually considered adequate for them. For industrial companies, total interest payments in each year examined should be covered at least three times by available earnings each year.

These are annual minimums and consistency is important. It means little if an industrial company's interest coverage soars to 10 times in, say, two particular years but is below the three-times minimum in the other years. The most reassuring five-year trend is one where the coverage meets the minimum standard each year and gradually increases over the period. Almost as acceptable is a stable picture in which there are small variations in available earnings year to year but the minimum standards are surpassed each year. However, a declining trend in coverage, even from an original high figure, is always a warning that further checking is needed. It is not conclusive in itself but it should never be ignored. Note also that any sudden steep drop in profit or a dip into the red should also be investigated immediately. There may be a good temporary reason, such as a strike, and the company's long-term financial health may not be damaged. Frequently, however, that is not the case.

As well as being reasonably sure that interest requirements will be met, a bond investor needs some reassurance that a company will be able to repay its bonds as they mature. This is necessary even if you do not intend to hold on to your bonds until they mature. Any adverse change in the probability of ultimate repayment will cut the price you can get for your bonds, often dramatically.

One test used is to calculate the company's annual cash flow from its operations as a percentage of its total debt for each of the past five years. The annual cash flow is almost always a larger figure than the company's net profit. Dig out the annual report again and look for the statement of changes in financial position, sometimes called the statement of cash flow. Look for the line that tells you how much cash came into the company from its operations, then compare that with the net profit on the bottom line of the income statement. The odds are they will be different, with the net profit usually smaller than the total cash flow. This is because accountants deduct bookkeeping items of various kinds from the company's cash earnings before figuring the bottom-line profit. These items are added back to the net profit to arrive at the actual cash flow. They include such deductions as depreciation and amortiza-

Measuring a Company's Financial Strength

Ratio of cash flow from operations to total debt =

$$\frac{\begin{array}{c}\textit{Cash flow from operations} \\ \textit{(including noncash deductions from profit)}\end{array}}{\textit{Total debt outstanding (short and long term)}} \times 100$$

Ratio of debt to equity =

$$\frac{\begin{array}{c}\textit{Total debt outstanding} \\ \textit{(including short and long term)}\end{array}}{\textit{Book value of shareholders' equity}} \times 100$$

TABLE XII

tion, deferred income taxes and any minority interest in the net profit. You get the total debt figure from the balance sheet. You should include both short-term and long-term debt (see example in Table XII). This calculation, too, should be done for the most recent five years.

Again, there are different minimum standards for utility and industrial companies. For the former, the annual cash flow from operations should be at least 20 per cent of total debt in each year. The annual cash flow from operations of industrial companies should be at least 30 per cent of total debt in each year. As with interest coverage, an improving trend is reassuring and a stable picture is acceptable. A declining trend should flash a warning signal.

Another important test is the debt-to-equity ratio. This is a measure of how much a company owes in relation to the book value of its shareholders' capital, or equity. You calculate this by adding up the company's short-term and long-term debt. Then you calculate this total as a percentage of its total equity. Again, the process should be repeated for the last five years.

The higher the percentage, the greater the risk that in bad times a company may not be able to maintain interest payments and meet its repayment requirements. However, because of their usually stable profits, utility companies are considered able to handle safely much larger quantities of debt than industrial companies. The rules of thumb for this ratio are maximums. For utilities, debt should not exceed more than 150 per cent of shareholders' equity. In other words, the company should not owe more than $1.50 for each dollar the shareholders have invested in it. The recommended maximum for industrial companies is a much smaller 50 per cent — that is, 50 cents owed for each dollar of equity. In each case, common shares rather than preferred shares should make up a high proportion of the equity (see Chapter 14).

Asset coverage is a less important test, but some government regulators insist on its use in prospectuses, the information documents that sellers of new corporate bonds are required to publish and make available to potential buyers. It is true that without enough assets such as plant and equipment to generate earnings, a company may fail to keep up interest payments and fail to repay debts when due. However, the actual value of assets usually becomes relevant only if a company is in danger of going under. At such a time, the realizable value of the assets will frequently be much less than their value on the books of the company.

For this calculation, only tangible assets, those you can touch, are taken into account. Balance sheet items such as deferred charges and goodwill are classified intangible and should be deducted from total assets. Then the total current liabilities are deducted from the result to arrive at net tangible assets available to back the company's bonds. This figure is then divided by the company's total long-term debt. The result is the number of dollars of net tangible assets for each dollar of debt. Again, utilities have to meet an easier rule-of-thumb test than industrials. They should have at least $1,500 of net tangible assets for every $1,000 of debt. Industrial companies should have more, at least $2,000 for every $1,000 of debt.

Clearly, this is a lot of work and it is easy to make a mistake doing it. The results of these calculations are only a starting point for a complete analysis. Professional analysts make many more checks of a company's financial statements when they assess the credit risk in buying some of its bonds. They also take into account the same sort of intangible factors that stock analysts use to judge how the company will do in the future. These include the demonstrated quality of the management, developments in the industry, competitive threats and a host of other difficult matters.

Few individual bond investors will find it worthwhile to tackle much of this sort of thing. Of course, you may be fortunate enough to have a large portfolio and also be intrigued by the intellectual exercise. If so, may all your do-it-yourself ratings turn out to be accurate.

CHAPTER 12

In the Bond Jungle

IN THE WORLD OF THE STOCK and bond markets, liquidity is not a measure of how much you drank at lunch. It is one of the principal benefits offered by an organized market: the ability to buy or sell with ease, and whenever you choose. We have grown used to the idea, but it still remains extraordinary that it is possible for you to pick up the phone, give an order to your broker to sell some shares or bonds and in most cases have that instruction carried out and the price confirmed almost immediately. Normally, to sell something of considerable value requires a period of advertising and negotiation, and you may have to wait quite some time before an interested buyer shows up. Remember the last time you sold your house?

The market for a bond or a stock is said to have good liquidity if it can absorb a reasonable amount of buying or selling with reasonable price changes. Opinions differ, of course, about what is reasonable. Disgruntled customers and harried brokers often disagree on that point. Nevertheless, the level of liquidity of any particular bond or stock is usually pretty clear. It depends on two main things: whether there is enough of the particular security in existence and available for trading, and whether there is sufficient interest among investors in it. Alert readers will notice that there is a chicken-and-egg question here. There is unlikely to be much liquidity in a particular bond until investors have become interested in it, and investors are unlikely to become interested until it has developed considerable liquidity.

Some bonds, notably those issued by the Canadian government, have a head start on liquidity because there are so many of them. Recently, Ottawa had some $275 billion of marketable bonds outstanding. As discussed above, Canada bonds have the highest credit rating of Canadian issues. Beginning investors can find virtually any term they fancy in this array and would be well advised to choose their first marketable bond investment from among them. Some of the issues are more liquid than others, and your broker should be able to identify them. Price and yield quotations are more readily available, and the trading spreads are somewhat smaller than on other bonds, so your cost of acquisition will be a little lower.

The terms on Canada bonds are also usually simpler and easy to understand. They rarely carry the bells and whistles that often adorn corporate bonds. The trade-off is that the yields on Canada bonds are lower than those on comparable bonds of provincial governments and their agencies (such as hydro utilities) and on corporate bonds. The difference varies from time to time, but it is always there.

Sometimes Government of Canada bonds may be retractable, which means that although the bonds have an official maturity date you can turn them in for cash at an earlier date. The converse of this is an extendible bond, which means you have an official maturity date but you have the right to keep the bonds for an additional period of time at a stated interest rate. Such bonds are issued when market conditions make it difficult to sell bonds on simpler but less favourable terms for the buyer.

Bonds issued by major provinces such as Ontario and Quebec, together with their hydro authorities, are also traditionally good credit risks. They are almost as liquid and offer a higher return than Canadas. Still higher returns are available on bonds of the smaller provinces but they are not as liquid and easy to buy or sell. This is even truer for bonds of municipal governments and their agencies, with a few exceptions. Moreover, the credit ratings of municipal bonds vary considerably and must always be closely watched.

The key to success in investing in bonds of the smaller provinces and of municipalities of all kinds is to find a broker who specializes in them. In several provinces, for instance, there is a lively and active market in municipals that you can plug into as an individual investor. Most of the time you will get a slightly higher return on municipals than you would on comparable term deposits or guaranteed investment certificates. You are not locked in, either, because you can usually sell small quantities of such bonds in the market at a reasonable price.

One peculiarity of municipal bonds is that many of the smaller municipalities issue so-called instalment or serial debentures. With these, a part of the issue is repaid each year over its life. For exam-

ple, a million-dollar deal might be repaid in instalments at the rate
of $100,000 over 10 years.

In several provinces, a provincial government agency raises
money for municipalities by selling bonds on their behalf. The provincial guarantee of interest and repayment of capital encourages
investors to accept a lower rate of interest than they might otherwise do. In other provinces, there may be no legal guarantee by the
provincial government of municipal government bonds, but the government keeps tight control on municipal finances and its approval
is usually required for bond issues. Unlike the federal and provincial governments, municipalities are generally not permitted to
carry over a financial deficit from one year to the next. This does
not prevent them from ever getting into financial trouble, but it is
reassuring.

Corporate bonds potentially offer the highest yields, although
yields on some top-quality corporates are often lower than those on
some lower-rated provinces and municipalities. Assessing them can
be a more complicated business because of the variety of terms and
conditions under which they are offered. Investing in corporate
bonds is suitable only for individual investors who are prepared to
earn the higher return by paying close attention. Dilettantes are
likely to run into trouble.

Normally, a company borrows money from the bank in the normal course of business for periods of up to a year in order to finance
day-to-day operations. Money borrowed for longer periods is raised
under a different arrangement. The technical term for the debt incurred is funded debt. The cash is generally used to buy assets that
will last for some time — such as land, buildings and equipment.
Money raised by taking on longer-term debts is also sometimes used
to repay short-term bank loans and other short-term debts incurred
perhaps for working capital.

Borrowing money is a cheaper way for companies to raise capital
than selling new shares because the interest is tax-deductible and
dividend payments are not. In other words, companies pay their interest bills with pretax dollars but dividends on company shares are
paid out of after-tax dollars. Why, then, do companies sell new
shares from time to time in order to raise capital? It is because they
have to balance off the cheaper debt financing against the commitments they take on both to pay a usually fixed rate of interest and
eventually to repay the money by a specified date. If business turns

bad, and these commitments cannot be met, the company will be in danger of bankruptcy. In contrast, dividends can be suspended any time at the discretion of the company's directors with no risk of starting bankruptcy proceedings, and most types of shares do not have a fixed repayment date.

The ultimate security behind any corporate bond is the business success of the company that issued it. However, various forms of legal security back up different companies' promises to meet their commitments. A company may identify some or all of its fixed tangible assets and put a first mortgage on them. If it defaults, bond owners have the legal right to seize those assets and sell them to get their money back, ahead of other less-secured borrowers. That right is usually exercised through the trustee of the bond issues, normally a trust company. The trustee also usually has legal powers to keep an eye on what the company does with its assets in order to make sure the bond owners' security is not weakened. Another form of this is the collateral trust bond, where repayment is backed up by depositing other corporate securities of higher credit quality with a trustee.

Bonds whose repayment is not secured by the pledge of particular identifiable assets are known technically as debentures. The company promises to pay interest and repay the face value of the bonds when due, but if it fails to do so, debenture owners have no claim against specific assets. Their security is the general credit of the company, and as creditors they rank behind owners of any mortgage-backed bonds.

This does not necessarily mean that a debenture always has a lower credit rating than a mortgage-backed bond. Many companies have sufficient financial strength and are well enough regarded to be able to raise money through selling debentures without having to pledge any particular company assets. Other companies sell debentures because of the nature of their business, which means they have few assets suitable for pledging. The fixed assets of some companies may not be available to be pledged as security because they have already been pledged to secure earlier bond issues. To complicate matters further, there are debentures that are partly secured by assets not sufficient to provide full coverage. These are known as secured debentures.

You will also often see references to subordinated debentures. Such debentures rank behind other securities or debt of the company. Exactly where the owners of these debentures stand can be discovered only by detailed research in the prospectus for their original sale or from reference sources such as The Financial Post Corporation Service. You may also run across corporate notes, which are usually unsecured promises to pay and which rank behind every other lender to the company. There are variations on this theme that do provide some specific security, however.

Researching the details of the specific security behind a bond is a job for experts such as the credit-rating services and is rarely done directly even by big-dollar investors. The important thing to remember, in any case, is that the best legal protection ever devised rarely provides much comfort for owners of the bonds of a company that fails financially. The land and buildings of a bankrupt company are hardly ever worth much in a liquidation. It is the earning power of a flourishing company that produces the cash needed to pay interest as promised and to meet debt obligations as they fall due.

Individual investors would do well, however, to understand the features of different corporate bonds and debentures that make investing in them a tricky business. Most notorious of these is the call feature, which gives a company the advantage of a two-way bet against the investor. It works this way.

Quite naturally, a company raising money through selling bonds wants to pay as little interest as it can for as short a period as possible. A bond buyer's desire is the reverse: to receive as much interest as possible for as long a period as possible. A company issuing bonds seemingly commits itself to paying today's going interest rate for the lifetime of the bonds. If interest rates then go up, the company's management is perfectly happy to go on mailing out the interest cheques they originally promised.

But what if interest rates go down? The owners of the company's bonds are happy because they are getting more interest on their money than they could if they bought new bonds. In addition, they have a nice capital gain on their investment because bond prices rise when interest rates fall. The company's management is not at all happy, though. They are paying out fat interest cheques to bond owners and looking longingly at the cheap money available in the bond market today. Can the company do anything about this? Indeed it can, if its management had the foresight to put a call, or redemption, provision into the original issue. This gives the company the option to purchase its bonds compulsorily from their owners on certain terms.

The traditional form of call did provide modest recognition of the injustice that exercising this privilege can cause. Companies set the call prices at the time of the issue and usually made them higher than the face value of the bond. Often there was a sliding scale with bigger premiums paid for early redemption than for late redemption. This reflected the reality that calling bonds shortly before they are to be repaid is no great hardship, but doing so earlier on is.

As the ups and downs in interest rates became bigger and more frequent, the premium prices frequently did not compensate investors sufficiently. Eventually a marketplace revolt forced changes in the standard call provisions. Today's call feature often gives the company the right to redeem bonds at any time but the price is set by a formula and changes with market conditions. The result of this so-called doomsday call is more reasonable compensation to investors whose bonds are called away from them. In addition, the new terms do not put a cap on the market price of the bonds if interest rates fall.

Retractable and extendible bond provisions are the mirror image of call provisions at the option of the company. As owner of a retractable 15-year bond, for instance, you have the right to hold on to it until maturity, but in five years' time you might be able to demand your money back early. Naturally, you would probably do that only if the going interest rate on similar bonds at the time was higher than the rate on the bond you own today. An extendible bond is one that has a maturity date of, say, five years but which allows owners at that time to hang on to their bonds for a longer period, perhaps at a different interest rate specified when the bonds are originally sold. You would naturally keep the bonds if the going rate on similar bonds at the time was lower. These bonds provide buyers with a two-way bet against the company. They are usually offered only when the bond market is in a hostile mood and long-term bonds cannot be sold on more normal terms.

There is another way in which you may be relieved of your corporate bonds against your will. This happens where there is a sinking fund provision in the terms. The company undertakes to set aside money from earnings each year in such a fund and hand it over to a trust company. The money is enough to repay all or part of the issue before it matures. Each year a fixed amount is used to buy in bonds, usually for their face value and not for a premium price. Companies do this to avoid the financial strain of having to repay the bonds all at once when they mature.

For the owners of sinking fund bonds this works like a lottery. The trust company hired to handle fund purchases will try to buy enough bonds at the prescribed price on the open market. If this attempt fails, however, the trust company picks by lot the numbers of bonds to be purchased. If you own any of the ones chosen, you will lose them, frequently for less than their market price. This suggests it might be a good idea to swap sinking-fund bonds that are trading at a premium price for others not in that category.

An alternative arrangement is a purchase fund. Under this arrangement, a specified amount of bonds is bought back each year, but only if the purchases can be made at or below a price fixed at the time of issue. This can serve as a support to the market price. There is also usually no provision for compulsory call of the bonds.

From time to time some companies sell what is known as a convertible bond. This hybrid creature is partly a loan to the company and partly an option on its common shares. Its owner gets the right for a period of time to exchange it for new common shares of the company at a price fixed at the time of issue, which is usually above the market price of the shares at the time. Frequently, the specified conversion price rises over time, a feature designed to encourage early conversion. Companies issue convertibles to borrow money more cheaply than they could otherwise. This method may also enable them to raise equity capital on more favourable terms than through selling shares directly.

Convertibles are sold to buyers with the argument that they combine the greater security and income of a bond with the opportunity to share the company's business success through a rising share price. There is something to this, but not much; it is mostly an illusion. Convertibles are rather like those all-purpose tools that don't do any particular job as effectively as a single tool designed for the purpose.

In the first place, you give up some income by buying a convertible. They always pay less interest than a comparable bond that does not have the conversion privilege. That is the price you pay for the call on the stock. If the company does well, you would probably do better buying the stock in the first place because you would pay less for it than from converting the bond. If the company does

Calculating the Conversion Cost Premium and Payback Period On Convertible Bonds

Here is how to calculate how much more it will cost you to buy a company's common shares indirectly through buying a convertible bond first, and how long it will take to recover the difference from the higher yield on the convertible.

1. Price of $1,000 debenture of XYZ Corp., convertible into 50 common shares, is $1,250.

2. Market price of XYZ common shares is $22, so 50 shares would cost $1,100 if bought directly (50 x $22).

3. Buying 50 shares indirectly through the convertible costs $1,250. So conversion cost premium is $150 ($1,250 - $1,100), or 13.6 per cent ($150 as a percentage of $1,100).

4. Years to pay back premium equal:

$$\frac{\% \ premium}{convertible \ yield - common \ yield} = \frac{13.6}{8 - 4.3}$$

$$= 3.7 \ years$$

TABLE XIII

badly, you will own a bond whose security will be no greater than that of a comparable bond without the conversion option but with a lower yield. Convertibles are also usually callable at small premiums, and most have sinking funds.

One thing to watch out for is a forced-conversion provision. This allows the company to call its bonds for redemption after the shares trade at or above a specified price for a certain period of time. A period of notice permits owners of the convertible bonds to exercise their right to exchange them for shares, which naturally they will all do. This provision can put a cap on the market price of the convertibles once the market price of the shares rises above the conversion price.

Typically, when the market price of the company's shares is considerably below the conversion price, a convertible bond behaves in the market in similar fashion to straight bonds of comparable quality and paying a similar interest rate. However, as the share price approaches the conversion price, the convertible may acquire a premium price, reflecting the prospect of being able to convert profitably. If the share price moves above the conversion price, the prospects for the company's stock become the dominant influence on the price of the convertible. It should sell for a price equal to the number of shares you get for each $1,000 bond multiplied by the share's market price, plus a premium. For example, if the stock is selling at $25 and you get 50 shares for each $1,000 bond, the convertibles should trade for at least $1,250 each ($25 times 50) and probably more.

An important calculation for investors considering convertible bonds is the payback period. Ignoring taxes, a convertible provides more income than the dividend on a company's stock. But buying the stock indirectly through the convertible costs more than buying the stock directly in the market. How long will it be before the higher return on the convertible fully offsets the premium price for the stock? The way to calculate this is explained in Table XIII.

Another common type of bond investment is the strip. This is created by dealers out of high-quality federal and provincial government bonds by separating some or all of the interest coupons from a bond certificate. The coupons, which are promises to pay fixed amounts of interest on a future date, are sold separately from the so-called bond residue (also known as a zero-coupon bond), which is a promise to pay the principal amount when due, plus whatever interest coupons were not stripped. Because money in the future is worth less than money today, the coupons and the residue are sold initially at discounts from their face value. Like regular bonds, their market price varies as interest rates rise and fall but usually in much bigger swings. Their price will, however, gradually rise toward their face value as the time for payment of the face amount approaches.

The main advantage of strips for an investor is that they eliminate what experts call the reinvestment risk. When you buy a regular bond, you get regular payments of interest, which you can spend or reinvest. The standard calculation of your return on your investment in the bond assumes that you are able to reinvest the interest at the same rate when you get it. Frequently, this isn't so. Interest rates may be higher then, in which case your effective return will be higher. They may also be lower, which will reduce your effective return. Buy a strip bond, however, and there are no interest payments to be reinvested. So long as you hold on to the strip until it matures, and so long as you get your money back then, your return is fixed at the start. You can see how important it is, though, to buy strips of an issuer with a high-quality credit rating.

There are three principal disadvantages. Strips may occasionally be difficult to sell before maturity because they are not traded on stock exchanges and there is no guarantee of a continuous market. In addition, the absence of regular interest payments helps make their market prices much more volatile. When interest rates rise, strip prices fall further and faster than regular bond prices, and vice versa.

Also, the taxman has a nasty surprise for unaware buyers. Even though you don't actually receive any income from your strip bond each year, he figures that you do and that it is in the form of interest, not a capital gain. The entire difference between your purchase price and the amount you will get on maturity is treated as deemed interest, and you are required to report a proper proportion of it each year on your tax return. This catch makes strip bonds an unattractive proposition to taxable investors. On the other hand, they are very attractive to people with self-directed registered retirement savings plans. The tax shelter provisions of such plans mean you don't have to hand over to the government each year some of the money you haven't received yet (see Chapter 18). Investments through the plans are usually long-term in nature. You are not looking for regular income each year from them, and you can choose maturities that more or less coincide with your expected retirement date. Strips are one prime ingredient of a retirement investment portfolio.

Ever inventive, the investment business has also come up with various combinations of strip bonds with regular bonds. These are called accrual notes because in the first part of their life they do not pay out any interest. The interest accrues and compounds for a while, like a compound-interest savings bond or term deposit. Eventually, however, regular interest payments begin and continue to maturity — subject to one very important exception. These notes always give the issuer the right to call them in after a certain point, which it will certainly do if interest rates are lower at the time. In return for that privilege, the investor gets an above-market yield to start with.

CHAPTER 13

A Profitable Parking Spot

GOVERNMENTS, BECAUSE THEY usually spend more than they raise in taxes, have a voracious appetite for borrowed money. One of the ways they satisfy it is through the regular sale of short-term promissory notes to investors at a price somewhere below their face value. In the U.S., such notes of the federal government are, logically enough, called treasury bills because they are issued by the Treasury Department. Oddly, the same name is used for Canadian government notes even though there is no such department in Ottawa. Canada's equivalent is the Department of Finance.

More familiarly known as T-bills, these notes are a handy place for investors of all sorts to park their money while they figure out what else to do with it. They come mostly with original life spans of three months (91 days, to be exact), six months (182 days) and one year (364 days). Because there are billions of dollars' worth of T-bills that trade actively, you can pretty well choose the term of your choice up to one year.

T-bills do not pay interest as such. The difference between your purchase price of, say, 98.50 and their par value of 100 provides the return or yield on your investment (see sample calculation in Table XIV on the next page). If you still own them at the time, you get paid the full face value when they mature. As with strips, the taxman, is not baffled by this arrangement and firmly insists that the gain on your purchase is really interest and therefore taxable as regular income.

Most T-bills are bought and sold in large amounts by professional money managers. Banks have large holdings, which they can count toward their government-required reserves of assets. The bills come in denominations of $1 million, but also in smaller amounts ranging as low as $1,000. Financial institutions and stockbrokers have minimum-purchase requirements ranging upward from $5,000. You buy

How To Calculate the Yield on a Treasury Bill

$$Yield = \frac{100 - price}{price} \times \frac{365 \times 100}{term}$$

So, if the price is 98.50 and the term 91 days, the yield is:

$$\frac{100 - 98.50}{98.50} \times \frac{365 \times 100}{91} = \frac{1.50}{98.50} \times \frac{36,500}{91}$$

$$= 6.11\%$$

TABLE XIV

T-bills like bonds, not stocks. The price you pay includes a profit and commission for the seller, and the price you get if you sell before maturity reflects a discount for the same purpose.

The yields available on T-bills closely follow the ups and downs of interest rates in general. Unlike longer-lived securities such as bonds, they do not lag behind a general rise in rates. Conversely, their yields do not trail behind a general fall in rates. Their principal use is as a temporary place for money from which you get a decently competitive, but not spectacular, rent.

Investing in T-bills can also pay off if you expect interest rates to rise soon and you want to keep your powder dry for that event. In the fixed-income market this is what investment experts call "going short." You commit your money for only a short period at today's yield in the expectation you will be able to charge a higher rent for it shortly. You also may do this if you really don't have any idea whether rates will go up shortly, stay the same or plunge, which happens even to experienced professionals more often than you might think. The opposite manoeuvre of "going long" involves making a longer-term commitment of your money at today's rate because you expect rates will soon be lower. By doing this you lock in today's higher rates while the going is good. Note that this kind of going short has nothing to do with the similarly named stock market manoeuvre of selling short – borrowing shares and selling them at today's price in the belief that the price will be lower soon and you will be able to make a profit from buying them back more cheaply.

The market yields on T-bills play an important role as an indicator for the entire Canadian financial market. That is because of the way a weekly auction of new federal government T-bills is handled. This closely watched event is managed by the Bank of Canada, and it usually takes place on Tuesdays.

The Bank of Canada is not a commercial bank. It is a semi-independent government agency charged with various responsibilities, but mainly with the supervision of the country's money supply and banking system and with acting as Ottawa's financial agent. Managing the national money supply is not as simple as you might think because money comes in many different forms in addition to the currency notes and coins with which we are familiar. Exactly how it is done is a complicated and highly technical subject of interest mainly to specialists. However, one aspect of it is both visible and sometimes controversial. It is the setting of the Bank of Canada's own lending rate, or bank rate.

This is not an interest rate that will ever be charged to you or me. It is the minimum rate charged by the Bank of Canada on loans it makes now and then to the country's commercial banks and certain other financial institutions and money-market dealers. These loans are to tide a borrower over a temporary shortage of cash that arises because of the unpredictable daily ebb and flow of money through the banking system. In addition, however, the Bank of Canada's rate is seen by the financial markets in general as a sort of master's voice. If the rate rises steadily, it is generally understood that the national monetary managers want to see interest rates rise in general. If the rate falls, the opposite signal is flashed.

The Bank of Canada does not, however, do anything as crude as simply announce the rate. What it says is that its rate will be set each day in close relation to the call loan rate, which is the interest rate at which banks lend each other money overnight. At the same time, the Bank of Canada can – and does – influence the call loan rate through its control over the banking system. In turn, it also keeps a watchful eye on the weekly auction of T-bills. Clearly, if there is keen demand for the government's new T-bills, the yields on them will tend to go down. If buyers are reluctant, they will have to be enticed by higher yields. Like many things in the money market, though, this auction is not quite what it seems. It is, to a considerable extent, rigged.

For a start, only a limited number of players can bid at the auction. Certain banks have the privilege, along with certain investment firms specializing in the money market. In return for the profitable opportunity of bidding at the auction, these firms assume the responsibility for maintaining a continuous market in T-bills and money-market securities of all kinds. This arrangement also puts heavy pressure on these highly competitive business rivals to accept and play by the Bank of Canada's rules.

There is an additional player: the Bank of Canada itself. It both runs the auction and reserves the right to bid, afterward and in secret. It is as if the auctioneer could invite bids, then close the auction and go into a back room and decide whether to top them himself. On the morning of the T-bill auction, the outside bidders assess the market, the outlook for interest rates and how many of the new T-bills on offer they would like to own – six-month and one-year bills as well as the three-month variety. Around midday, they send a message to the Bank of Canada's people with their bids. Between 12:30 p.m. and 1:30 p.m., the Bank of Canada broods on the bids, and a few minutes after 1:30 p.m. it announces the results of the auction.

Clearly, this system provides the Bank of Canada with the opportunity to influence the level of T-bill rates. For the outside bidders, the operation is a multimillion-dollar poker game. They know for sure only what they themselves are bidding, although they may pick up some idea of what others are bidding in the game of bluff and counter-bluff that goes on over the phone in the hours preceding the auction. The Bank of Canada, in contrast, is in the position of a player that gets to see everybody's hand before making its own bids. If the bids that come in will produce an average yield higher than it wants, the Bank of Canada can support the auction with its own bid.

Federal government T-bills are the principal merchandise traded in the Canadian money market, but many other kinds of securities with short lives change hands there. The market exists because idle money is wasted money. For example, a corporate treasurer may find himself with surplus cash in the company's bank accounts, which will not be needed until next Thursday. So instead of letting it sit there, he makes it available for rent in the money market and earns a decent rate of interest. Or the treasurer of a finance company that lends money to customers to help pay for their new cars may find she is running a little short of cash to meet the demand. So she rents some in the money market, charging the customer a good deal more rent, of course. Banks find themselves with more money in the till at the end of the day than is needed right away, so they do the same thing as the corporate treasurer with surplus cash on his hands. At other times, a bank may emulate the finance company treasurer and tap the market for needed money.

It all adds up to a lot of money put to useful work each day and a more efficient financial system and economy. Annual trading amounts to more than a trillion dollars. The way the market works, with millions of dollars changing hands on the strength of a telephone conversation, all the major participants must have high credit ratings. A bounced million-dollar cheque anywhere along the line can cause serious problems. There is nothing to stop you, however, from putting your surplus cash to work in the money market instead of having it sit idle – so long as you have quite a bit to spare and you are not in the habit of issuing dud cheques.

As well as federal government T-bills, you can buy bills issued by several provincial governments. These offer a higher return than Ottawa's bills, but remember that this reflects the somewhat higher credit risk. A bigger problem than the remote possibility of not getting your money back is that they are not quite so easy to buy and sell as the federal bills because the market is not quite so liquid. Short-term federal government bonds maturing in three years or less are also considered part of the money market rather than the bond market. By definition they are of equal credit quality to federal T-bills, but they are less liquid.

Your broker may also have available the promissory notes of finance companies, known as finance company paper. These outfits finance the sales of consumer products such as cars by borrowing money with one hand and lending it to the buyers with the other. For example, the major car manufacturers all have financing subsidiaries that support sales this way. If you borrow money through your dealer to swing a purchase, this is where it usually comes from. Returns on this paper are higher than on Ottawa's T-bills and in some cases the minimum-purchase requirement may be just $10,000. The paper may be secured by specific assets such as the instalment payments of customers, or it may be backed by just the general credit of the issuer. Remember that it is possible for a car company and its finance subsidiary to go broke, so keep your eyes and ears open if you invest in this stuff.

Major corporations with top credit ratings also issue promissory notes for large amounts, backed by lines of credit from their bankers. This is known as commercial paper. Other companies with decent credit ratings issue promissory notes called banker's acceptances because they carry a backup guarantee of payment by a bank. These are mainly places for parking large sums of money, used mostly by big-time professional money managers. The minimum-purchase requirement is typically $100,000 or more.

Yields on money-market securities rise and fall with supply and demand and the general pattern of interest rates. Normally, the return on your investment is lower than you could get on longer-term securities with perhaps a greater credit risk. However, from time to time yields on short-term money-market securities are higher than on longer-term securities (see Chapter 10). Mostly, though, the money market offers a reasonably safe parking place for your surplus cash, and pays you for the privilege.

CHAPTER 14

Are Preferreds Preferable?

IT MAY NOT BE TOO FAR along in your career in fixed-income investing before somebody suggests preferred shares as an ideal purchase. Think carefully before you accept the suggestion. Used with a clear understanding of their advantages and disadvantages, preferreds can be a useful and profitable addition to your portfolio. Too often, however, investors in preferred shares do not really know what they are getting into. They think of preferreds as a corporate bond under another name, paying fixed dividends instead of interest and offering certain tax advantages. This is a dangerous misunderstanding.

The first thing to note is that when you buy a company's preferred shares, you do not become a creditor of the company. You become a part-owner, just like the purchasers of the company's common shares. Check the company's balance sheet and you will find its preferred shares classified as part of its shareholders' equity, not of its debt. This also means that your investment usually has no time limit on it and no promise of repayment by the company, with some exceptions.

The principal consequence of this status is crucial. The owner of a preferred share does not have a legal right to demand continued payment of promised dividends. At their discretion, a company's directors can stop payment of dividends at any time, and they often do when bad times hit. The directors even have a legal duty to stop paying dividends in some adverse financial circumstances, whether they want to or not. In contrast, failure to make promised interest payments to a creditor has immediate legal consequences and can lead eventually to bankrupting the company. No company has ever gone bankrupt merely because it failed to pay dividends on schedule, although that often marks the first step on the road to ruin.

Naturally, a company with preferred shares in the hands of investors makes every effort to avoid failure to pay promised dividends on common and preferreds alike. The stock market punishes such corporate embarrassments severely. Normally, non-voting owners of preferred shares may also get voting rights if dividends are not paid for a long enough period, usually two years, and there may be a provision to pay dividends that are in arrears. But there's no getting away from it — dividends are paid out of bottom-line profits, and if there aren't any profits a company may have no alternative but to stop paying dividends.

This risk raises big questions about whether fixed-income investors should consider preferreds at all. If the income from an investment is going to be fixed, there should at least be very good odds that you are going to keep on getting it. This, of course, is the heart of the matter. Companies also do default on their bonds if disaster strikes and the legal remedies available to the owners of those bonds are not all that attractive. The first and last question every fixed-income investor must always ask is how good are the prospects of receiving the promised income. If the prospects are good, it does not matter all that much whether the income comes in the form of interest or dividends — except after taxes, where dividend payments may have an edge.

It can be argued that for an individual taxable investor, the favourable tax treatment of dividends is the only reason for buying preferred shares to provide income. In most circumstances, you will have to hand over to the government more cents out of each dollar of interest than out of each dollar of dividends or capital gains (see Chapter 18). In the case of dividends, this recognizes the probability that the company paying the dividends has already paid corporate income tax on the money, for dividends are paid out of after-tax profits. Interest is paid out of pretax income, and is deducted by the company as an expense on its income-tax returns. Note that the company does not have to be actually paying tax for this treatment of dividends to apply, just that it be potentially taxable in Canada if it makes a taxable profit. Dividends from foreign companies do not get this special treatment.

The mechanism for delivering this tax break is a peculiar creature known as the dividend tax credit, which applies to dividends on common and preferred shares alike. You take the amount actually paid and add 25 per cent to it, called "grossing it up." The resulting amount — $1.25 for each dollar of dividend paid — is called the taxable amount of dividend (see example in Table XV). You in-

Calculating the Dividend Tax Credit

Canadian resident in federal tax bracket of 26 per cent receives $1,000 in dividends from a taxable Canadian corporation. Here is how the dividend tax credit and after-tax income are calculated.

1. Start with actual dividend amount	$1,000
2. Gross up dividends by 25% ($1,000 x 0.25)	250
3. Calculate taxable dividend amount	1,250
4. Calculate federal tax ($1,250 x 0.26)	325
5. Calculate federal tax credit ($1,250 x 0.1333)	167
6. Calculate federal tax payable (subtract credit)	158

All provinces except Quebec		Quebec residents	
Federal tax payable	$158	Federal tax due	$158
7. Provincial tax	$74	Federal abatement (16.5%)	-$26
(e.g., 47%)			
		Federal tax payable	$132
		Provincial tax	$325
		Provincial credit ($1,250 x 0.0887)	-$111
		Provincial tax payable	$214
Total taxes payable	$232	Total taxes payable	$346
Net dividend	$768	Net dividend ($1,000 - $346)	$654
($1,000 - $232)			

Note: Federal and provincial surtaxes not taken into account.

TABLE XV

clude this amount in your net income on your tax return and calculate what you owe the federal government in the normal way. But then you reduce the result by subtracting the dividend tax credit, calculated outside Quebec as 13.33 per cent of the taxable amount of dividend. In all Canadian provinces except Quebec the final step is to apply the correct provincial rate to the net federal tax as reduced by the dividend tax credit.

Life is more complicated for Quebec investors because the province runs its own separate system of income taxes. The process of calculating tax on dividends is the same up to the point where the net federal tax owing has been reduced by the 13.33 per cent federal dividend tax credit. Quebec taxpayers then reduce their federal tax bill by a further 16.5 per cent and are liable to Ottawa only for that amount. To satisfy the provincial government, taxpayers first calculate their net income according to Quebec's different rules and then add the grossed-up amount of dividend income ($1.25). The provincial tax bill is calculated in the normal way, but it is then reduced by a provincial dividend tax credit (8.87per cent of the grossed-up amount).

Don't be dismayed, though. Making use of the dividend tax credit is not usually as complicated as it sounds. If you receive dividends, you should get an annual statement from each company showing the grossed-up amount and the amount of the dividend tax credit. Quebeckers get two statements from each company, one for the federal amounts and one for the provincial amounts. You just put the numbers in the right boxes on your tax return and do the calculations by following the instructions on the return.

The effect of the dividend tax credit is to make a dollar of dividends worth more after taxes than a dollar of interest. At first blush, therefore, you might think that taxable fixed-income investors would always choose dividend-paying preferred shares over interest-paying investments. They don't, for two main reasons. Number one was mentioned earlier: the somewhat greater security of interest payments over dividend payments, other things being equal. The second reason is more important but less obvious to beginners. Investors are not fools, most of the time. The financial markets always adjust to reflect differences in tax treatment. Because dollars of dividends are more attractive than dollars of interest after tax, taxable investors are willing to pay more for a dividend-paying investment. Considered the other way around, investors will accept a lower pre-tax yield on a preferred share than on a term deposit or bond. In mid-1996, for example, you could get 7 per cent on five-year term deposits. At the time, average yields on good quality preferred shares ranged from 6.5 to 6.75 per cent. There would be no sense to this if the tax rules did not treat dividend income more favourably than interest income.

Most of the time, in fact, the gap between those different investments is larger for another reason. In many cases, taxable Canadian companies can receive dividends from other taxable Canadian companies free of tax. Their appetite for good quality dividend-paying preferred shares frequently raises the price and lowers the yield to levels that make them unattractive to individual taxable investors.

Like corporate bonds, preferred shares come in many different flavours, with widely varying conditions. You can discover what these are for a particular issue from the standard reference sources (these are listed in the bibliography). You will find the promised dividend stated either as a fixed dollar amount or as a percentage of the par, or stated value, of the shares. The dividend on an issue offering an 8 per cent dividend might be described as $2, which is 8 per cent of each share's $25 par value, or simply as 8 per cent. Note that the original issue price may not be $25. It is frequently discounted a little to raise the effective return to the original buyer. The market price of the shares will also vary afterward, in a similar fashion to marketable bonds. If interest rates in general rise, prices of preferred shares will in general fall. If rates fall, preferred-share prices will usually rise.

One of the most important things to be sure of is whether the promised dividends on a particular preferred share are cumulative or non-cumulative. The former is better than the latter and most preferreds are in that category, but better to be safe than sorry. A cumulative feature means that if a company decides to stop paying preferred dividends, the unpaid amount is not forgotten about. The dividends accumulate as arrears, and these must all be paid in full before the company can resume paying dividends to owners of its common shares and before it can redeem the preferred shares. A non-cumulative preferred does not offer this prospect. Once unpaid, a dividend on that type of share is gone forever, just like an unpaid dividend on a common share.

Notice that arrears are paid to those who own the preferreds at the time of repayment, not to those who were owners at the time the dividend was first cancelled and who have since sold their shares. So buying cumulative preferred shares shortly before a company resumes paying dividends or decides to redeem them can be very rewarding. This sort of thing is not really fixed-income investing, however. It is a speculative investment and more akin to playing the stock market.

You should also check call or redemption provisions. As with bonds, these can mean that you lose your preferreds just when their price is rising because interest rates are falling. The company wants to pay off its preferred shares and raise money by borrowing at a lower cost. You will get a small premium over the par value of the shares if that happens, but it is often not enough to compensate for the lost opportunity. In addition, you will be faced with reinvesting the money you receive for your shares, probably for a lower return.

Sinking funds and purchase funds frequently accompany preferred shares, again like bonds. The trust company handling the sinking fund uses money set aside by the company to buy back a specified amount of preferred shares each year, enough to retire all of the issue over a period of years. If it is not able to buy the required quantity at the specified price, usually the par or stated value, it will call in shares by lot. This does provide some support for the market price but it can also mean that you have to turn over to the company some or even all of your investment at a below-market price. A purchase fund does not have that drawback for preferred shareholders because there is no compulsory purchase provision. The trust company merely tries each year to buy the specified amount of shares at the prescribed price. This also provides some support for the market price.

Voting rights can be important from time to time. Unlike the owners of common shares, preferred shareholders usually do not have the right to vote on the selection of directors and other matters that come up at a company's annual meeting. This is because most managements believe preferred shareholders should have no say in the company's affairs so long as the promised dividends are paid. A common provision grants voting rights to owners of preferred shares after a certain period in which dividends are not paid, often two years. Such a provision also frequently guarantees that the preferred shareholders will be able to elect a certain number of directors in such circumstances.

Preferred shareholders do usually have a right to vote as a separate group on company moves that affect either their position relative to other shareholders or the financial backing behind their shares. In compensation for their fixed dividends, which unlike common-share dividends usually do not rise if the company does well, owners of preferred shares rank ahead of common shareholders in their claim to assets if the company does badly and is liquidated. However, both types of shareholder rank behind creditors. So some issues provide that in certain circumstances the approval of a certain proportion of preferred shareholders is required before the company sells more bonds or creates more preferred shares. Some issues also restrict the payment of dividends on common shares — for example, if the payment would reduce the company's working capital below a certain amount.

Sometimes the approval of a certain majority of preferred shareholders is required for the company to dispose of a large proportion of assets or to undertake a major corporate reorganization.

Companies can usually change the terms of preferred shares after they have been issued, but special procedures are almost always required to ensure that such changes are not made without the consent of a clear majority of the owners of the shares.

The ingenuity of companies and their financial advisers has produced several variations on the preferreds theme. You will, for instance, find retractable preferreds. These give their owners the right to force the company to redeem the shares on a fixed date at a specified price. In effect, this creates a maturity date for the shares and makes them more like a bond.

If the market price of a retractable preferred matches or is below the retraction price, it is important to calculate the pretax yield the proper way. In those circumstances, it is highly likely the shares will be retracted at the first opportunity. The yield-to-maturity method designed for bonds should therefore be used (see Chapter 8). That method should also be used if a retractable preferred is trading above its call price, to recognize the probability that the company will redeem the shares as soon as it can. If, however, a retractable is trading above its retraction price, it is highly unlikely that shareholders will ask for their money back when the time comes. Therefore, the regular dividend yield calculation should be used. The annual preferred dividend should be calculated as a percentage of the market price.

Other variations of less interest to investors seeking a fixed income can be found. They all violate, in one way or another, the maxim that you should keep things simple. They include:

Convertible preferreds: These usually give owners the right to swap their preferred shares for common shares of the company at a specified price for a specified period of time. For fixed-income investors, they are open to the same objections as convertible bonds. The dividend is lower than on a comparable straight preferred, in return for the prospect of making capital gains on the company's common shares if it does well. In the latter circumstance, you might do better buying the common shares directly. The same is true of preferreds that come with warrants to buy common shares of the company at a fixed price for a certain period of time.

Floating-rate preferreds: The dividends on these are not fixed in advance. They generally go up and down in line with interest rates, but usually between a specified floor and ceiling. Naturally, the floor will be well below interest rates at the time of sale and the ceiling will be well above. The dividend is often linked to the prime lending rate of a major bank, for example. There can even be delayed floaters, where the dividend is fixed for a while and then starts to vary with interest rates. The terms of these shares insulate you from the dangers of rising interest rates but also from the benefits of falling rates. Their market price is affected only slightly by rising and falling rates.

Participating preferreds: This variety gives their owners the right to share in a company's business success by offering a fixed dividend plus additional dividends that depend on profits. A company might promise $2 a year to its preferred shareholders. Then, after common shareholders have received a similar amount, the two classes of shareholders might be entitled to share equally in additional dividends. There may also be limited participation rights for preferred shareholders. Whether this sort of preferred share is worth its price is a tricky call. You have to take into account both the yield provided by the fixed dividend and whether there are good prospects that the company will be able to pay bigger dividends down the road.

Foreign-pay preferreds: A few Canadian companies, including the big banks, offer preferred shares that pay dividends in foreign currency, usually U.S. dollars. These work out well if the currency rises in value against the Canadian dollar, but rather badly if it goes down. They can be used, however, to provide some insurance protection against a plunge in the Canadian dollar. In addition, their dividends still qualify for the dividend tax credit.

The bewildering array of possible conditions attached to preferred shares should never blind you to the single most important question: Will the company continue to pay dividends? As with bonds, one simple way is to check whether the quality of the issue you are being offered is rated by Canada's two rating services (see Chapter 11). If so, what is the rating? Any broker should be able to tell you. Make sure you understand where a particular rating ranks, though. They range all the way from super-safe to high-risk speculation.

Calculating Preferred Dividend Coverage

$$\text{Coverage} = \frac{\begin{array}{c}\textit{Net income (before extraordinary items)} + \textit{minority} \\ \textit{interests} + \textit{income taxes (current \& deferred)} + \\ \textit{total interest charges}\end{array}}{\begin{array}{c}\textit{Total interest charges} + \textit{total preferred dividends} \\ \textit{(adjusted for income tax*)}\end{array}}$$

$$\textit{*Dividend adjusted for tax} = \frac{100}{100 - \textit{apparent tax rate}}$$

TABLE XVI

Professional analysts working for the two services put the finances of a company whose shares they are rating through a rigorous analysis. They also try to keep track of changes in its prospects and adjust the ratings if necessary. This does not mean they are always right, merely that you will have someone to blame if things go wrong. The professionals are sometimes caught by surprise, too.

Serious buyers of preferred shares should cross-check the professional ratings with some do-it-yourself tests. The most important of these is the preferred dividend coverage test. By how much does the company's profit available for preferred dividends exceed the amount required for those dividends? To find out, you check the net income before extraordinary items shown in the company's most recent annual report. You add back to it any minority interest deducted, all income taxes (current and deferred) and the total interest charges. This total is then divided by the total interest charges plus total preferred dividends adjusted for income tax. The tax adjustment is needed because dividends are paid after taxes but interest payments are paid before taxes. You therefore have to gross up the preferred dividends to an equivalent basis (see example in Table XVI).

Preferred dividend coverage should be calculated for the past five fiscal years of the company, if possible. The trend is important, not just the figure for a single year. Rule-of-thumb minimums are two times coverage for utilities such as natural gas distributors and telephone companies, whose profits are usually pretty stable, and three times coverage for industrials, whose profits generally fluctuate more. Below those minimums, the risk of an interruption in dividend payments is fairly high. The further above them, the less the risk is. The test should not be applied mechanically, however. Investing is always a matter of balancing risk and reward.

A second important test for a fixed-income investor is the company's record of continuous dividend payments. If it is long, that is a reassuring factor. If there have been several interruptions, that is a warning signal you will ignore only at your peril.

A recently introduced kind of investment vehicle is becoming a popular choice for investors seeking higher income payments, and who are temperamentally and financially able to take on some business risk to that income. What you buy are units in a trust specially created for this purpose. The trust receives a share of the cash earned from the production and sale of such natural resources as oil, natural gas, iron ore or coal. After their initial issue, the units are listed on a stock exchange and can be bought and sold like stocks. The trust pays out the income it receives, less some minor expenses, to owners of the units — usually quarterly, but monthly in some cases.

Although generally known as royalty trusts, there are actually two different types. One is the royalty trust itself. This type receives its income in the form of a royalty. Certain tax breaks given on natural resource production mean that for a number of years the trust's income is tax-sheltered. In turn, that means that the income paid out to its unitholders is tax deferred. Unlike interest or dividends, that income does not have to be included in the investor's taxable income at the time. However, the distributions usually reduce the adjusted cost base of the units (see Chapter 18). This increases any eventual capital gain or reduces any capital loss that may eventually be realized.

The second type is more properly known as an equity trust. This kind of trust receives the income from natural resource production in the form of interest and dividends. In turn, the income it distributes counts as interest or dividends, depending on its source, and the unitholder is liable for tax on these payments each year according to the normal rules (see Chapter 18).

As income investments, the market value of both kinds of unit rises and falls in the opposite direction to interest rates, like preferred shares. Unlike preferreds, however, the income is not fixed. It always starts off high but it will fluctuate with the price of the natural resource involved. That is why these units should be classified as equity investments, not fixed-income investments.

The other thing to keep in mind is that the income you get comes ꓱxisting natural resource deposits. This means that, in a sense, part of the income is a return of your capital. This suggests you should look for an organization behind the trust with a good record of finding and developing new resources, or a trust with a claim on natural resource reserves stretching far into the future. Some notable examples of the latter are the Alberta oilsands and Labrador's iron ore.

CHAPTER 15

Becoming a Mortgage Lender

LENDING MONEY TO PEOPLE who want to buy a house is a huge and profitable business. Financial firms such as banks and trust companies do it on an enormous scale. They borrow money from savers with one hand, advance it to house buyers with the other, and get their profit from the difference between the interest they pay and the interest they get. Repayment of the loan is secured by a mortgage on the house. If the owner doesn't pay, the lender or mortgage holder can seize the house and sell it. Usually that covers the mortgage, even though the owner's investment may be wiped out. It's much more fun than borrowing the money and struggling to keep up the mortgage payments.

So if you have accumulated a considerable pile of savings and want a good and reasonably safe return on them, why not become a mortgage lender yourself? Well, you can. There is, however, a tough way to do it and an easy way. To understand the attractions of the latter, it's first necessary to understand the difficulties of the former.

The tough way is to cut out all the middlemen, except perhaps a mortgage broker, and in effect go into the mortgage lending business yourself. That way, you get to keep all the interest the borrowers pay, less some operating expenses and any bad debts. Note the last proviso: The expenses will be minimal but write-offs could hurt badly. The do-it-yourself approach can be rewarding, but if you don't pay close attention you can get into a lot of trouble, mainly because you will be operating on a small scale compared with a bank.

The standard Canadian house mortgage is arranged so that the lender gets monthly payments of interest and principal. These are calculated to provide full payment of the mortgage at maturity, typically in 20 to 25 years. This process is called amortizing the mortgage. Note that the borrower begins to pay off the loan from the first payment, although in the early years he might hardly notice the principal portion. Most of the monthly payments will consist of interest (see example of a payment schedule in Table XVII). This is what gives homeowners with a large mortgage the feeling that they are getting nowhere fast. For mortgage lenders, in contrast, the arrangement is highly satisfying. Financial companies normally limit themselves to lending up to 75 per cent of the value of the property at the time, and that's a good rule for you to follow as well. Assessment of the value should be done by a professional real estate appraiser. Don't rely on the municipal evaluation.

This restriction provides a cushion for the lender if real estate prices drop. It should also ensure that the borrower himself has a sizable investment in the property, which is a deterrent against merely walking away from the deal if things get tough. Typically, that would happen at a time of falling real estate prices when it might be difficult to sell the property for the remaining amount owing on the mortgage. There are schemes that enable purchasers to borrow as much as 90 per cent of the value, but these rely on government-sponsored insurance to cover the risk to the financial company on the excess amount above 75 per cent. They are not for you as a small-scale mortgage lender.

You should also stick to first mortgages, at least in the early stages of your career as a mortgage lender and perhaps always. That means you are first in line to seize the property if the owner doesn't pay the mortgage. Second and third mortgages may offer alluringly high interest rates, but in a default they put you second or third in line and there may be nothing left to pay the balance owing to you. You need a lawyer or notary to make sure that you really are first in line. There may be other legal claims registered against the property that the borrower did not know about, forgot about or merely neglected to mention. Houses can burn down, so you need to make sure the owner has adequate fire insurance paid up to date. Houses can also be seized by the local municipality for unpaid property taxes, so you have to make sure those are paid, too.

Clearly, do-it-yourself mortgage lending is a tricky business. Your principal problem is that your mortgage portfolio is likely to be highly concentrated. You are not likely to reap the benefits of diversification enjoyed by a big financial company with a huge portfolio. If only one house in your town burns down without fire insurance in force, but it's the one on which you hold the mortgage, you have a big problem. For a bank, that's not great news either but it is just one house among many on which it holds mortgages.

A Mortgage Amortization Schedule

First payment date:	July 31, 1992
Principal borrowed:	$100,000
Term in months:	300
Beginning interest rate:	9%
Payment:	$827.98
Total interest paid:	$148,393.22

Payment number	Payment date	Interest portion	Principal paid	Principal balance
1	31-Jul-92	$736.31	$91.67	$99,908.33
2	31-Aug-92	$735.64	$92.34	$99,815.99
3	30-Sept-92	$734.96	$93.02	$99,722.97
4	31-Oct-92	$734.27	$93.70	$99,629.27
5	30-Nov-92	$733.58	$94.39	$99,534.88
6	31-Dec-92	$732.89	$95.09	$99,439.79
7	31-Jan-93	$732.19	$95.79	$99,344.00
8	28-Feb-93	$731.48	$96.50	$99,247.50
9	31-Mar-93	$730.77	$97.21	$99,150.29
10	30-Apr-93	$730.06	$97.92	$99,052.37
11	31-May-93	$729.33	$98.64	$98,953.73
12	30-Jun-93	$728.61	$99.37	$98,854.36
13	31-Jul-93	$727.88	$100.10	$98,754.26
14	31-Aug-93	$727.14	$100.84	$98,653.42
15	30-Sep-93	$726.40	$101.58	$98,551.84
~~	~~~~~~	~~~~~~	~~~~~~	~~~~~~
290	30-Aug-16	$64.19	$763.79	$7,954.11
291	30-Sep-16	$58.57	$769.41	$7,184.70
292	30-Oct-16	$52.90	$775.08	$6,409.62
293	30-Nov-16	$47.19	$780.78	$5,628.84
294	30-Dec-16	$41.45	$786.53	$4,842.31
295	30-Jan-17	$35.65	$792.32	$4,049.99
296	28-Feb-17	$29.82	$798.16	$3,251.83
297	30-Mar-17	$23.94	$804.03	$2,447.80
298	30-Apr-17	$18.02	$809.95	$1,637.84
299	30-May-17	$12.06	$815.92	$821.93
300	30-Jun-17	$6.05	$821.93	$0.00

TABLE XVII

If you still want to go ahead to earn interest that is typically 1 to 1.5 percentage points above the going rates on guaranteed investment certificates, there are mortgage brokers who are in business to put borrowers together with lenders. You find them under Mortgages in the Yellow Pages telephone directory. Some lawyers and notaries do the same thing or know people who do it. As a lender, there should be no fee or commission for this service; the borrowers normally pay. You can also find people looking for mortgage money in the classified ad sections of newspapers.

The easy way to rent out your savings in mortgages is through one of Canada's best-kept investment secrets: mortgage-backed securities, or MBSs for short. Another name for them is Cannie Maes, which is a ripoff of the name Ginnie Maes, the nickname for the Government National Mortgage Association certificates commonly used in the U.S., where they have been around for many years and are available in large quantities. Your usual source for mortgage-backed securities is a broker, although some banks and trust companies offer them as well. You buy and sell them like bonds, at prices that take into account a commission on the transaction.

What you buy is a stake in a large pool of residential mortgages. These mortgages all come with a government-backed guarantee of payment of principal and interest, given by the Canada Mortgage and Housing Corporation. Each month, the issuer pays interest at the rate promised, plus a payment of your share of principal repaid by the borrowers. It's as if you held the mortgage yourself, except that the interest portion of the payment you get is a little less than you would get directly because of deductions to cover expenses and fees. However, you are better off because you get your monthly payment of mixed interest and principal even if some or all of the borrowers fail to make payments. What's more, this guarantee is not limited to a maximum dollar amount, unlike government deposit insurance. Whatever the amount you buy, you do not have to worry about the quality of the mortgages in the pool or the financial health of the outfit that put the pool together.

The investment comes in $5,000 units. You must buy a minimum $5,000 to start and additional units must always be that same size. Depending on market conditions, you may be able to buy your $5,000 units at a discount price. Alternatively, you may have to pay a premium price. Income tax is payable on the interest portion of your monthly payments but not on the portion that is a repayment of your loan. The units can usually be held within registered retirement savings plans and registered retirement income funds. You should check the information circular giving details of the issue to make sure.

Each pool stands alone and has its own interest rate and maturity date. Mortgage-backed securities were originally required to have a life of at least 4.5 years and most issues were for a standard five years. Because a majority of Canadian mortgage borrowers prefer shorter terms of much less than five years, growth of these pools was limited. In 1990, however, the minimum life was reduced to six months. Now you can usually choose from maturities of one year to 20 years.

Monthly payments are a prime attraction of mortgage-backed securities. They arrive automatically around the middle of each month. You do not have to keep track of payment dates or clip bond coupons. However, depending on the type of mortgage pool, you may get a larger than usual payment in some months. Many mortgages allow the borrower to make additional principal payments on top of the scheduled payments, usually on the anniversary date of the mortgage. Some pools consist of such prepayable mortgages, while others don't. In the former case, your share of any prepayments is passed along to you with the monthly payment. You also get your share of any penalty interest payments made by the borrowers, perhaps resulting from early prepayment. This is a bonus you weren't counting on when you made the original investment.

These arrangements do pose the problem of reinvesting the principal payments received. It is vital to avoid forgetting that these are not interest payments; they are repayments of part of your original capital. When your $5,000 unit eventually matures, you will not get back $5,000. You will get that amount less the principal you have already received. If you have spent the repaid principal, your capital will have been reduced to that extent. Make sure you put the principal repayments back to work immediately, if at all possible.

Another attraction is that there is a market for your mortgage-backed securities if you want, or need, to turn them into cash before they mature. You can ask your broker to sell them at the going price, like a bond. That price will depend on what has happened to interest rates since you invested in the securities. If rates have gone up, the price you get will be less than you still have invested, after allowing for principal repayments. No one is going to be willing to pay full price for securities offering less than today's interest rates. More promisingly, if interest rates have gone down, you should get more than you originally paid, less any principal repayments. Your higher-rate securities should command a premium price.

Like all markets, the actual price will reflect supply and demand. Prepayments further complicate things. You usually get a higher yield on pools of prepayable or open mortgages to compensate for the uncertainty of not knowing for sure the size of each monthly payment. So long as you buy your units at the original price of 100 cents on the dollar, early prepayments do not affect that annual yield. They do shorten the term of the investment, however. In other words, you receive the promised return for a shorter period of time than you thought.

If you buy in at a discount price, though, prepayments increase the effective yield on your investment. That's because you get the full amount of the principal back earlier, and a dollar today is always worth more than a dollar tomorrow. The opposite is true if you buy in at a premium. You paid that premium price to get a stream of above-average interest payments over a certain period of time. If that stream ends prematurely, your effective yield is less than it would have been.

In any case, the difference between what you paid and what you get will be a capital gain or a capital loss. One interesting manoeuvre is to buy low-rate resale securities at a discount and hold on to them until they mature. You may even be able to sell them for a good profit before maturity if interest rates come down. Even though you do have to pay capital-gains tax on them, the rate will be less than you have to pay on ordinary interest (see Chapter 18).

Should you go for mortgage-backed securities in preference to term deposits and guaranteed investment certificates? Only if you want or need monthly payments. The certificates are simpler to understand and offer highly competitive interest rates so long as you do not want a monthly cheque. If you do, the interest rate will be lower and all of the cheque will be taxable at your highest rate. There is also virtually no possibility of making a capital gain on your deposits or certificates.

Mortgage-backed securities are more difficult to understand when you first encounter them. You must realize from the start that part of the monthly payment is a return of your capital, and make every effort not to fritter it away. They do, however, offer competitive rates of return with a minimum of fuss and bother, guaranteed fully by taxpayers in general as a result of the government guarantee. Don't rule them out for your fixed-income portfolio.

CHAPTER 16

Hiring the Pros

SUPPOSE YOU WANT TO RENT out your money for more than you can get through your average savings account, term deposit or investment certificate, but you have neither the time nor the inclination to learn enough to do it directly yourself. A solution to this is to hire professional investment managers by investing in a mutual fund. These funds pool the money of their customers and invest it on their behalf. The cost of the professional management and the overhead is split among all the customers, so your share will be small.

Investment funds have been around since the dawn of the investment business. They get the money they invest by selling shares or units. Their profits, if any, come from the interest and dividends they get on the securities they hold, plus any capital gains made from trading the portfolio. A mutual fund is a particular and popular variation on the theme. Unlike closed-end funds, a mutual fund's shares or units are on sale continuously. That is why it is called an open-end fund. Its size is not fixed but changes from day to day as money flows in or out.

In addition, an investor in a mutual fund can sell shares — also known as units — back to the fund at any time. This right of redemption is the distinguishing feature of a mutual fund. It ensures that there will always be a close relationship between the redemption value of its shares and their market value.

Mutual fund shares are priced at their net asset value, which changes with the market valuation of the securities in the fund's portfolio and the number of unredeemed shares or units it has sold. The net asset value per share (NAVPS) is published in the financial pages like stock and bond prices. It is calculated this way by the fund: Add up the total assets of the fund, including cash and its portfolio holdings at market value. Subtract the fund's total liabilities. Divide the difference by the number of unredeemed shares or units sold.

One quirk of mutual funds is that not all the money you hand over may be put to work for you. Many funds levy a sales charge on each purchase and that charge may be deducted before your dollars are invested. This is called front-end loading. Theoretically, it can go as high as 9 per cent of your investment in the first year, but this is a maximum laid down in the fund's rules. The percentage is negotiable and is usually discounted heavily in today's highly competitive markets. A fund must disclose its sales charges and volume discounts in its prospectus, which is a public document available to all investors. Most of this money goes as commission to the sales representatives who secured you as a customer, although some may be held back to help pay for promotion of the fund. You pay a front-end load only once, of course. Unlike a stock, you don't pay twice — when you buy, and when you sell.

Some funds, particularly those sold by banks and trust companies, are no-load funds — that is, they don't have sales charges. You can't expect much assistance in deciding on your investments at a bank branch, however. Some sales representatives for front-end-loaded funds provide good service and advice. Others don't. Investors looking for help with their fund investments should shop around and be prepared to pay for it if they find it. Those who don't want or need advice will probably do better with a no-load fund.

There's always a catch, though. Some back-end loaded funds may not have any sales charge up front but hit you with a hefty charge if you cash in during, say, the first six years. You won't be able to negotiate these fees, either. Some funds even charge you commission when you buy and a redemption fee when you cash in. Some allow you to move your money from one fund to another in the same group free of charge. Others charge a fee for the privilege. All funds also charge an annual fee for the professional investment management they provide, usually in the form of a percentage of the market value of the assets being managed. The money is charged against the fund and reduces the investment return on your money.

All these fees must be disclosed in the fund's prospectus. Their total impact is reflected in the so-called management expense ratio, which usually includes everything except direct sales charges and registered retirement savings plan trustee fees and is also published in the prospectus. This ratio varies from as low as 0.75 per cent to more than 3 per cent. The typical range is 1 to 2 per cent. To encourage their investment managers, some funds pay performance incentive fees on top of the basic fees. This is money you could save by doing your investing yourself. However, if you don't have the time or interest, it is money well spent.

Just as with renting your money out directly, you have a choice of funds that buy bonds, money-market securities, mortgages or preferred shares. People who invest in such funds are willing to give up the prospect of big capital gains for being able to sleep at night without worrying about what's happening to their savings. The managers of fixed-income funds put safety of capital ahead of risky growth. Bond-fund managers keep most of the assets in high-quality government or government-guaranteed bonds. Any corporate bonds they buy will be those of large companies with strong balance sheets and high credit ratings. The managers of money-market funds are heavily into government treasury bills. The mortgages in fund portfolios are almost universally first mortgages, which give the fund first claim on the assets if the borrower doesn't pay. Fund managers try to buy top-rated preferred shares where there is little risk of the company failing to pay the dividend. Of course, there can always be surprises in investing, but there are likely to be fewer of them if these policies are followed. The important thing to remember, however, is that no mutual fund offers a guaranteed fixed return, no matter how it is invested.

You keep track of how you are doing by checking the net asset value per share of your fund in the listings in the newspaper financial pages. Performance is measured by the difference in net asset value per share at the end of a period with the start of a period. As always with comparisons of performance, you should compare apples with apples and do this over a long enough period to evaluate consistency, say, five years. Be careful when comparing fund performance with a stock market index. Most such indexes do not reflect reinvestment of dividends. The total return indexes of the Toronto Stock Exchange are an exception. They do take account of reinvested dividends as well as price changes.

It is not always easy to navigate among the various claims made by the sponsors of money-market funds about the yields they offer. In Canada, you might find that a fund advertising a seemingly above-average yield is using a so-called "effective yield" method, which is considered misleading and is not allowed under U.S.

rules. The more straightforward "current yield" approach is required south of the border, and most Canadian sponsors use it as well. Setting aside the intrinsic merits of either method, what you should always do is make sure that any yield comparisons you rely on to choose a fund are made on the same basis.

For example, in the summer of 1990 when rates were high and money-market funds were hot items, one Canadian bank advertised a yield of 13.29 per cent the same day that a competing bank advertised 12.64 per cent. Had the bank with the seemingly lower rate used the same method of calculation as its rival, however, its yield of 13.39 per cent would have handily topped its competitor's yield. The higher figures are produced by using the "effective yield" method. This technique involves taking an average yield on the fund's portfolio for as little as one day, or perhaps over seven days, then compounding the figure monthly or quarterly for 12 months. The "current yield" method produces a lower figure by taking the income earned by the fund over a seven-day period, multiplying it by 365 days and then dividing the result by seven. There are arguments for both methods and neither is fundamentally wrong. The important point is not to compare results produced by one method with results produced by the other method. Make sure your comparison shopping is based on results produced only by one of the calculation techniques. It's easier these days because many funds now publicize their yields calculated both ways. In mid-1996, typical money-market funds were showing 3.9 per cent current yield and 4.1 per cent effective yield.

The net asset values of funds go up and down in similar fashion to the prices of the securities in which they are invested. However, fixed-income funds usually offer a smoother ride than funds that invest primarily in the stock market. Naturally, since fixed-income funds are designed principally to earn interest, the changing level of interest rates in general has the major impact. When interest rates rise, their income from new investments also rises but the market prices of their existing investments fall. The result is usually a decline in the net asset values of bond and preferred-share funds in particular. Similarly, when interest rates drop, their net asset values rise. The managers of these funds also try to anticipate swings in interest rates. They adjust their portfolios to profit from the changing environment and avoid big losses.

Mortgage-based funds are generally less volatile. They do suffer capital losses when interest rates rise, because the market value of the mortgages already in their portfolio falls. This is partly offset by the higher interest on renewals or new mortgages they acquire. Their portfolios almost always consist of a mixture of short-term and longer-term mortgages. These days, also, there are very few mortgages maturing in more than five years, unlike the large number of 15-year to 20-year bonds on the market.

The least volatile funds are those invested in savings deposits or money-market securities. Most such funds are priced at a fixed value of, say, $1 or $10. The interest earned on your money is used to buy additional units for you. Savings funds usually do better than you can through direct investment because they deposit money in large amounts and earn considerably higher interest. The managers of money-market funds also do better than you could do directly for the same reason. When they buy treasury bills in large amounts, they get a better deal than when you buy $10,000 or $25,000 at a time. They also have access to the more complicated big-dollar securities such as banker's acceptances and short-term promissory notes issued by large corporations with high credit ratings, which generally offer more interest than your regular retail-size term deposit.

Most fixed-income funds are qualified investments for your registered retirement savings plan (see Chapter 18). If not tax-sheltered in this way, however, you are liable for tax each year on the income and net capital gains they earn on your behalf, even if you don't actually receive it. In effect, the tax rules regard a mutual fund as a sort of conduit through which the investment income and net capital gains are passed along to you. To levy tax on the mutual fund would, therefore, involve double taxation. Fund organizations are required to send their customers a yearly statement of such potentially taxable income, which you use when you prepare your tax return.

CHAPTER 17

Graduating
to Leverage

HOW TO MAKE ONE DOLLAR
do the work of several is the graduation course of investing. It's
called using leverage and it's the way really big money is made in
the world of finance and investment. Although you may have forgotten your classroom lessons in mechanics, you make use of physical leverage frequently in the everyday world. The most common
and dramatic demonstration occurs the day you have a flat tire. To
change the wheel, you have to lift a one-tonne car some distance off
the ground. How does any one person do that? With a mechanical
jack and a piece of firm ground to stand it on. The jack, a sophisticated form of lever, magnifies its user's physical strength many
times. So does the wrench used to loosen the wheel nuts. Opening a
can? The can opener you dig out from the drawer operates through
leverage. Turning over the garden? Your spade works through leverage, too.

Some successful investors make frequent use of the financial
equivalent of leverage. Others steer well clear of it. If you use it, you
can magnify your profits dramatically. Be warned, though: Use it
unsuccessfully, and your losses will be equally as magnified. Just
like a car that falls off a jack can injure a careless mechanic, unwise
use of leverage can hurt you financially. Check out those really big
losses in the investment world and you will often find excessive
leverage was behind them.

Leverage is inherently less dangerous for a fixed-income investor
than a stock market investor, although it is much more difficult to
find an opportunity to use it. The former rents out money with the
working assumption that all of it will come back in due course, plus
interest. The latter buys a company's stock and then shares in its
business fortunes, for better or worse. There is a prospect of making
a lot more profit than a money-renter, but there is also a very real
risk of losing some or all of the original stake if things go wrong.

Financial leverage rests on borrowed money. It works this way. If you put $1,000 into a one-year term deposit at 10 per cent, your profit will be $100 and at the end of the year you will have $1,100. Now suppose you had borrowed an extra $1,000 and put a total $2,000 into the deposit, at the end of the year you would have $2,200.

What would your profit be after you repaid the borrowed $1,000? It depends on how much interest you had to pay out. If it was 10 per cent, the same as the interest paid on the deposit, you would be neither ahead nor behind. You would have $200 interest coming in and you would have paid out $100, leaving a net profit of $100. True, the interest cost would be deductible on your tax return but the interest income would be taxable. So your after-tax profit would normally be the same whether you borrowed an additional $1,000 or not.

Clearly, if it cost you more than 10 per cent to borrow the additional money, you would be behind on the deal. At a cost of 11 per cent, you would still receive $200 in interest but you would pay out $110, leaving you with only $90 profit instead of $100. But let's look at what happens if you were able to borrow the additional money at 9 per cent. After repaying the loan at the end of the year you will again have $200 interest in your account and you will have paid out $90 interest. Your net profit: $110 instead of $100. Now work through what happens if you were able to borrow $9,000 at 9 per cent and rent out a total of $10,000 for one year at 10 per cent. Your net profit after repaying the loan would be $190 instead of $100. The additional amount borrowed to make the investment greatly increases your gain in proportion to the size of the loan you take on and the leverage you employ.

Because the risk of not getting all your money back from a fixed-income investment is low, it is usually fairly easy to leverage your investment 100 per cent. You have $5,000 in Canada Savings Bonds, say, and $5,000 in cash. Normally, any banker will jump at the chance to lend you $5,000 against the security of your savings bonds, especially if you are going to put the $5,000 plus your own $5,000 into a term deposit at that bank. Most bankers will go for the deal even if you don't have any money of your own to invest to start with, so long as they are reasonably confident you will be able to re-pay the $5,000 loan from your own resources eventually. The banker is, in fact, not at risk at all if your savings bonds are pledged as security for the loan and are physically lodged with the bank.

Unhappily, however, it is rarely possible for you to borrow money at a lower cost than the interest available on low-risk fixed-income investments. That privilege is mostly reserved for banks and other financial institutions. Indeed, it is the basis of their business. They pay you rent of, say, 5 per cent for your savings deposits and lend out your money to somebody else for perhaps 8 per cent. They do this on a large scale, with a relatively small amount of their own capital to backstop the operation. Even after operating expenses and write-offs of bad loans that don't get repaid, it's a pretty good line of business to be in.

It is the prospect of rising dividends and capital gains that makes leverage a common and often profitable practice in the stock market. The same goes for investments in real estate. By definition, though, fixed-income investments do not offer the same possibility of a rising return on your money that will outstrip your borrowing costs. Standard financial leverage, therefore, is not widely used by individual money-renters.

There is a way of using borrowed money to apply psychological leverage to yourself, however. Many of us find it very difficult to accumulate an investment stake merely by voluntarily setting aside money as savings. There always seems to be something else on which to spend any money left over from daily living expenses. In such cases, borrowing a reasonable amount to build up your savings can make sense. This may seem an odd way to go about it. The object of saving your money is to increase your net worth. Taking on a loan does the opposite. It decreases your net worth until you repay it, and it costs you interest.

There is method to the madness, though. The technique takes advantage of human psychology. Once legally committed to repaying a loan in regular instalments, most people do follow through. Like payroll deductions, the payments become a habit and pass almost unnoticed, so long as they are not too large. In addition, people generally don't like to be considered financial deadbeats, and failure to make the payments required under the terms of the loan can have troublesome consequences for your credit rating.

You must be careful, though. Remember you are borrowing to increase your savings, not to go bankrupt. The best plan is to only take on a loan you are certain you can pay off completely over a year or, at most, over two years. Err on the side of caution when working this out. Try always to borrow on a secured basis, so as to keep the interest cost down. If you have savings bonds or term deposits already, use them as the security for your loan. The payroll savings schemes offered by many employers to help employees buy Canada Savings Bonds are ideal for this manoeuvre (see Chapter 6). Don't use credit-card advances; they're far too costly. Above all, once having paid off the loan, don't spend the money. Use it to earn interest and perhaps to back up another loan, to be repaid along the same lines.

How much can you borrow? Suppose you can pay $100 a month on a loan costing 10 per cent. Twelve monthly payments will pay off a loan of $1,138 completely, otherwise known in the financial trade as amortizing the loan. Each payment will be part interest and part repayment of principal. Because this is a short-term loan, all the payments will be mostly principal. The longer the term of the loan the smaller will be the principal portion in the early payments. Homeowners with a long-term mortgage will be familiar with this disheartening fact. Over two years, though, you could pay off a 10 per cent loan of $2,167 at $100 a month. Pay $200 a month and you could amortize a loan of $4,334.

Remember to deduct the interest cost on the loan from your taxable income if the money is used to make an investment. It's only fair because the interest earned from investing the borrowed money is taxable. Ask the lender for a statement of the interest you have paid. You can and should check the amount for yourself, remembering that it's not quite as simple as it might seem. In the case of the $1,138 loan over one year at 10 per cent, the answer is not 10 per cent of $1,138, or $113.80. It's less, because you are repaying the loan as you go. The first payment of $100 reduces the amount outstanding by approximately $91 and succeeding payments by larger amounts.

The correct way to calculate your total interest bill is to add up all your payments and subtract the amount of the original loan. The answer is the difference between the two. In this case, it is approximately $62. Calculating the actual proportion of principal and interest in each successive monthly payment of $100 is a much more complicated mathematical exercise. Fortunately, these days electronic calculators and computer software are available to do the job

Personal Loan Amortization Schedule

Amount borrowed: $1,138
Number of payments: 12
Interest rate: 10%
Monthly payments: $100.00
Total interest $62.55

Payment number	Payment amount	Principal portion	Interest portion
1	$100.00	$90.53	$9.48
2	100.00	91.28	8.72
3	100.00	92.04	7.96
4	100.00	92.81	7.20
5	100.00	93.58	6.42
6	100.00	94.36	5.64
7	100.00	95.15	4.86
8	100.00	95.94	4.06
9	100.00	96.74	3.27
10	100.00	97.55	2.46
11	100.00	98.36	1.65
12	100.00	99.18	0.83
Total paid	$1,200.00	$1,137.50	$62.55

TABLE XVIII

if you really want to know. Any lender should also be willing to supply the figures, too (see example in Table XVIII).

There are two other ways to use leverage on fixed-income investments. You can buy futures or options contracts, but this hardly qualifies as renting your money out. True, you make use of fixed-income securities such as government bonds, but your aim is not to earn interest. It's solely to profit from price changes — in other words, to speculate. The futures market, in particular, exists to shift price risks from those who don't want to incur them to those who do. The people who take on the risks do so in the hope of a huge gain on a small stake.

Futures and options are both known as derivative products because they exist only by piggybacking on something else: stocks, bonds, money-market securities, commodities, stock indexes. It is crucial to understand the fundamental difference between them, however. The owner of a futures contract has a legal obligation to buy, or sell, a rather large quantity of something on a fixed future delivery date. Most owners don't wait around until then. They pass the obligation on to somebody else by selling their futures contract in the market, preferably for more than they paid for it. Let your attention wander, though, and you could find yourself trying to put $500,000 of government bonds on your credit card.

In contrast, the owner of an option has a choice. The contract gives you the right for a fixed period of time to buy something, or sell something, at a price fixed in advance. You don't have to exercise your options. It's up to you. The come-on is the possibility of making a big capital gain on a small amount of money. It's a classic use of leverage, and it offers the attraction that your risk of loss is limited to your original stake, plus any commissions. Interestingly, though, most options buyers don't exercise and so lose 100 per cent of their stake. Your risk of loss is fixed in advance, but it's also highly probable. The main problem with options is that you have to get two difficult things right instead of one. You not only have to be right about the direction of a price change, it has to happen within a fairly short period of time.

For the loser in futures, things can get much worse. You can lose much more than your original stake if things go wrong. When you buy a futures contract, you put down a small deposit, which is what offers you the chance of leverage-magnified gains. If the price of the underlying security moves against you, however, you may be required to put up more money or be sold out. The trouble here is that the price of the futures contract may fall so fast that you cannot get out for days on end. The exchanges frequently operate a daily price limit, that is, the price of the contract is not allowed to move up or down more than a certain amount in a single day. This sounds comforting, but the protection is illusory. When the price-change limit is reached, even in the first 30 seconds after the session opens, trading halts for the day. In a fast-moving futures contract, this can go on for many days in a row. Of such torture is personal bankruptcy made.

The fact that most options expire unexercised suggests there could be an opportunity to profit from being on the other side of the deal. The buyer of a call option pays a fee, called a premium, for the privilege of backing his conviction that the price of the optioned security will rise. The buyer of a put option pays a similar fee for the privilege of backing his conviction that the price of the underlying security is about to fall. Those fees, less expenses and commissions, go to the original creators, or "writers," of the options. They can produce a steady flow of income over and above the interest or dividends earned on the underlying securities.

The technique of creating options on securities you already own is called covered writing. It is the only reasonably safe way to go about the options business. Options created on securities you don't already own are known as naked options for a reason. They are highly risky adventures verging on recklessness. If bond prices start to move in the direction the option buyers anticipated, you will have to deliver the securities when called on to do so. That means going into the market to buy them at the worst possible time, with prices moving against you.

Writing options on bonds is a game for experienced investors with substantial portfolios. You need to find a broker who knows the ins and outs of the game and handles the mechanics efficiently. The best opportunities for profit occur close to turning points in interest rates, when impatient speculators frequently anticipate a move in prices too early. As a writer of options, you want stable prices at a time when people are expecting prices to move soon. That way, there will be plenty of options written but few will be exercised, leaving you to cash in the premiums paid.

Large investors can also use the options and futures markets to hedge interest-rate risks. The professional managers of large investment funds mostly use them for this purpose, to shift the risk to speculators. The techniques used are often complicated and expensive, and are beyond the scope of a book on fixed-income investing by individuals. If you are interested in this sort of thing, you can obtain more information through your broker and from the stock exchanges where options and futures on fixed-income securities are traded.

CHAPTER 18

Dealing with the Taxman

INVESTORS HAVE A FINANCIAL partner in all that they do — a compulsory partner. It's the government, in its various guises. The savings you accumulate painfully may come from income that has already been taxed, but if you rent them out and make a profit on the arrangement, government tax collectors will frequently demand a piece of that, too. The real return on your savings is only what you get to keep after paying income taxes. Cheer up, though. There are legal ways to lessen or defer the tax bite into your profits from fixed-income investment.

From earlier chapters you know that fixed-income investors primarily seek to earn interest, although there are methods of renting out money that can produce capital gains or capital losses as well. All interest you earn is considered regular income, like your pay, and is potentially taxable now or later. However, in the interest of playing fair, the government allows you to subtract many of the costs you incur to earn interest and requires you to pay tax only on the net profit, if there is any.

For instance, you can deduct as carrying charges the cost of renting a safety deposit box in which to keep your bonds. Other deductible expenses include fees paid for investment advice. Most accounting fees related to your investments are also deductible except money paid to prepare your income tax return.

Of great importance to a fixed-income investor is the ability to deduct interest paid on money borrowed to earn interest. The general rule is that the interest is deductible so long as any eventual investment income is not exempt from tax. Clearly, this means you can safely deduct the interest charged when you buy Canada Savings Bonds through a payroll savings plan. You can also deduct the interest paid on a bank loan where the money is used to make any kind of interest-earning investment such as term deposits, guaranteed investment certificates, bonds of any kind, treasury bills or mortgages. Note, however, that the interest stops being deductible when you no longer have the investment and it is not replaced by another investment of at least the same amount as the loan.

What happens if in a single year you incur more interest and investment expenses than your total investment income in that year? You can still deduct it all and, in effect, use your investment losses to reduce your regular income.

Investors have to include in their net income just three-quarters of net capital gains — that is, after capital losses are deducted. They then pay income tax at normal rates on the increased taxable income.

The effect of this special treatment is that one dollar of income is not always the same as another dollar of income, depending on the source it came from. Investors should always be aware of this phenomenon. A dollar of interest is worth roughly the same after tax as a dollar in your pay. That same interest dollar is worth less after tax, however, than a dollar of capital gains. You never have to pay tax on at least 25 cents of the dollar of capital gains. Incidentally, the dollar of interest is also worth less than a dollar you receive as part of a dividend paid by a taxable Canadian company. The tax break on the dividend payment recognizes the fact that the dividend is usually paid out of the company's already-taxed profit. It is delivered by something called the dividend tax credit (see Chapter 14).

In short, you always get to keep more of a dollar of dividends or capital gains after paying your taxes than a dollar of interest or pay. How much more? Unhappily, today's unbelievably complicated tax rules ensure that there is no single and widely applicable answer. Your tax bill depends on your tax rate, which in turn depends on the amount of your taxable income from all sources. The tax rate is slightly different in each province, so where you live makes a difference, too. In Quebec, where you have to comply with federal rules and somewhat different provincial rules, different definitions of taxable income change things.

Some rough rules of thumb exist, though. It's fairly easy, for instance, to compare the after-tax return on dividends with the after-tax return on interest. What you get to keep out of a dollar of dividends after tax is approximately the same as what you get to keep out of $1.30 of interest. In other words, you have to receive about $1.30 of interest to match, after tax, each dollar of dividends.

1996 Equivalent Pretax Yields

If you live outside Quebec and your marginal tax rate is 51.36%*, your equivalent pretax yields in 1996 would be:

Interest	Dividend	Capital gain
4%	2.98%	3.16%
5	3.72	3.96
6	4.47	4.75
7	5.21	5.54
8	5.96	6.33
9	6.70	7.12
10	7.45	7.91

*Median federal and provincial/territorial marginal tax rate for taxpayers in highest tax bracket.

As a Quebec taxpayer with a top marginal tax rate of 52.94%* your equivalent pretax yields in 1996 would be:

Interest	Dividend	Capital gain
4%	3.07%	3.12%
5	3.84	3.90
6	4.61	4.68
7	5.38	5.46
8	6.14	6.24
9	6.91	7.02
10	7.68	7.80

*Combined marginal tax rate for taxpayers in highest tax bracket
SOURCE: RICHTER USHER VINEBERG

TABLE XIX

Calculating and comparing after-tax capital gains with dividends and interest payments is trickier. There are variations from province to province. In addition, it's worth noting that dividends bear a lower rate of tax than taxable capital gains, even after excluding 25 cents of each dollar of non-exempt capital gains from tax.

You might wonder why any money goes into interest-paying investments at all if the taxman always takes a bigger piece of the profits than from other kinds of investments. It wouldn't if the financial markets did not adjust to reflect the tax treatment of different forms of investment income. Taxable investors are always willing to pay more for a dollar of dividends than a dollar of interest. The market, therefore, puts a higher price on an investment that pays dividends than on an investment that pays interest, especially if it offers the prospect of rising dividend payments and capital gains too. In other words, a taxable investor is willing to accept a lower before-tax yield on a dollar invested in a stock than on the same dollar invested to earn interest. This is why in mid-1996, when you could obtain 7 per cent on five-year term deposits, the average yield on the dividend-paying stocks that make up the Toronto Stock Exchange utilities sub-index was only 4.6 per cent.

One way to go about making comparisons is shown in Table XIX. It provides a representative selection of pretax yields on interest, dividends and capital gains in 1996 that would produce about the same return after tax. For example, a person living outside Quebec with a top marginal tax rate of around 51 per cent would have to earn 8 per cent interest before tax in order to keep about 3.9 per cent after tax. To equal that, the person would need almost 6 per cent pretax in the form of dividends, and 6.3 per cent pretax in the form of taxable capital gains. In Quebec, a person in the top federal and provincial tax brackets would keep about 3.8 per cent after tax out of 8 per cent interest before tax. To equal that, the Quebecker would need 6.1 per cent before tax in dividends and 6.2 per cent before tax in taxable capital gains.

These calculations and comparisons ignore a further complication, the alternative minimum tax, or AMT. That's because tax experts are unable to supply any general rules of thumb to help figure out the impact on investment decisions of this Catch-22 device. Each case must be worked out individually because the possible combinations of circumstances are so varied.

The AMT is designed to make sure that nobody can legally escape paying tax on investment income entirely, even by making ingenious and enthusiastic use of legitimate tax shelters. First, you calculate your tax bill in the regular way. Then you calculate it under the AMT rules. This involves adding back to your regular taxable income certain so-called preference, or tax-shelter, deductions you have made. Next you subtract the basic exemption of $40,000 plus the gross-up amount on Canadian dividends (25 per cent). The minimum tax you have to pay to Ottawa is 17 per cent of the result. Quebeckers use 20 per cent on their provincial tax return and you can increase the $40,000 exemption within certain limits by certain tax-sheltered "strategic economic investments." However, in its

1996 budget, Quebec proposed to cut this exemption to $25,000 for 1997 and subsequent years.

If the result of this involved process works out to be less than your regular tax bill, you are home free. If it's more, you have to pay the larger AMT bill. This is not quite as bad as it seems, in one respect. You do get to carry forward for seven years aproximately the additional amount you are required to pay when your AMT exceeds your regular tax bill, and use it as a credit against your regular tax bill in a year when that bill is larger than the AMT.

Heavy indulgence in tax-sheltered investments makes you more likely to become subject to the AMT. So can large amounts of the 25 per cent tax-free portion of capital gains. The long list of such preference deductions that have to be added back to your taxable income also includes:

- Contributions to registered pension plans, registered retirement savings plans and deferred profit-sharing plans. For instance, you may find yourself liable for AMT if you save up your annual contribution room to registered retirement savings plans for a few years, then make a large catch-up contribution in one year.
- Half of the bonuses paid on Canada Savings Bonds.
- Tax-sheltered investments of many kinds, but only to the extent that the tax deductions taken produce losses.
- Interest expenses related to such tax-sheltered investments.
- For Quebec provincial taxes only, contributions to a Quebec stock savings plan.

The guides provided by the federal and Quebec governments with your annual tax return supply some calculations you can use to check whether you are likely to be subject to AMT. If you suspect you may be, you can try to wing it by obtaining the special forms available from taxation offices. It may be a smart idea to consult a professional tax adviser, though.

Today's investors face problems both in complying with all the tax rules that affect them, which get more complicated and obscure every year, and in taking advantage of the legitimate breaks provided by tax laws. In a never-ending attempt to plug loopholes, our governments keep changing the rules. Even professional tax experts have difficulty keeping up.

True, you can avoid most of the difficulties if all you ever do is earn interest on a savings account, term deposits, guaranteed investment certificates or government savings bonds. Even there, however, things can get tricky. From now on, for instance, you are obliged to report and pay tax each year on interest you have not yet received on compound-interest savings bonds acquired after 1989. The rule is the same for deposits and certificates acquired after 1989 and maturing in more than a year, even though you do not get interest payments until maturity. At one time you could defer doing that until the interest was actually received. Then you were allowed to defer doing it for a maximum of three years or until the interest was received.

Worse, confining yourself in that way for simplicity's sake can cost you a bundle in lower returns on your money. Renting your money out by buying marketable bonds can bring you lower-taxed capital gains, but it requires you to get acquainted with the complicated world of capital-gains tax rules. It's a tough choice, but with today's high tax rates it is worth making the effort. In some cases, for large amounts of savings, it will even be worth paying a professional adviser. Bonds selling well below their face value are particularly attractive to individual investors in a high tax bracket because much of the return from holding them to maturity will be treated as lower-taxed capital gains.

Usually, the sale or redemption of a marketable bond is considered by tax collectors to be a capital transaction producing perhaps a capital gain or a capital loss. However, if you do this kind of thing frequently and behave more like somebody operating a business enterprise, any profit from selling a bond for more than you paid for it may be considered fully taxable just like the interest. The consolation for this is that selling a bond for less than you paid for it would be fully deductible.

The kind of things tax collectors take into account include buying and selling many different bonds or bills over short periods of time, having special knowledge and experience of the financial markets, and investing primarily with borrowed money. If this profile fits you, and you do not want your capital gains to be fully taxed as ordinary income and you are not actually a professional trader or dealer in financial securities, you can probably head off this prospect by electing to have all gains and losses from sale of Canadian securities treated as capital gains or losses. This election is made on a special form and once you make it you can't change your mind later on.

Capital gains and losses are measured against the adjusted cost base of your bonds, which is usually, but not necessarily, the same as the price you paid. It consists of the original price plus any additional costs of acquiring the bonds, such as commission, but not interest paid on money borrowed to make the purchase. You subtract this adjusted cost from the sale price, then deduct any sales commission from the difference, and you have either your capital gain or loss. A complication arises with bonds because of the probability of accrued interest. Very frequently, bonds change hands between interest cheques. The seller of the bonds is entitled to the interest earned up to the date of sale but still unpaid, and the buyer pays it to the seller on top of the price. That payment is ignored when calculating any capital gain or loss on the transaction. The seller treats it as investment income. The buyer includes in investment income only the net amount of interest for that year.

Here is an example: An investor buys a $10,000 principal amount of a 7 per cent bond at 98 on June 23, 114 days after the last $350 semi-annual interest payment March 1, and so has to pay $218.63 of accrued but unpaid interest. The purchase price of $9,800 plus accrued interest of $218.63 is $10,018.63.

The buyer's adjusted cost base is $9,800, not $10,018.63. When he receives the next $350 interest cheque, he deducts the $218.63 of accrued interest he paid and reports only the net amount as income on his tax return. The seller reports the $218.63 as investment income and uses $9,800 to calculate her capital gain or loss.

It gets more complicated when identical bonds are bought and sold. You have to, in effect, calculate a new average cost for the total holding each time additional identical bonds are bought. An example should make the process clearer.

An investor makes the following purchases of Anderson Enterprises 8 per cent bonds:

Febr. 2: $20,000 principal amount at 95	$19,000.00
April 6: $10,000 principal amount at 92	$9,200.00
Total cost	$28,200.00

The same investor sells $10,000 principal amount at 97 on June 1. The capital gain is calculated this way:

1. Total cost of identical securities	$28,200.00
2. Total principal amount of identical securities	$30,000.00
3. Principal amount of identical securities sold	$10,000.00

4. Adjusted cost base of identical securities sold:

$28,200 divided by ($30,000/$10,000)	= $9,400.00
5. Proceeds from sale of $1,000 principal amount	$9,700.00
Less adjusted cost base	$9,400.00
Capital gain	$300.00
Taxable capital gain (75%)	$225.00

These rules apply to bonds acquired after Dec. 31, 1971, when the capital gains tax system began. There are different and more complicated rules for bonds bought earlier than that. If you have to figure out capital gains or losses on such bonds, you should probably talk to a professional tax expert.

Because interest is taxable as ordinary income and more heavily than dividends and capital gains, fixed-income investments are prime candidates for a tax-deferred shelter such as your registered retirement savings plan. Two things put you ahead of the game if you can defer tax on interest earned: Reinvesting interest you would otherwise have paid to the government earns you more interest; and when the tax finally comes due, you may be in a lower tax bracket.

Registered retirement savings plans take full advantage of these benefits. Money you put into a plan to make investments is deductible from your taxable income within certain limits. That means you are investing with before-tax dollars. Yet the profits you make on your investments are not taxable so long as they are kept within the plan and reinvested. You face taxes on the full accumulated amount of your original investments plus the profits when you cash in the plan, but you can defer that at least until the year in which you become 69. At that point you can also choose to start taking annual amounts of taxable income in the form of a lifetime annuity or from a registered retirement income fund.

You can have as many RRSPs as you want. You can choose so-called guaranteed plans where your money goes into savings accounts, term deposits or investment certificates. Government deposit insurance covers these plans within the normal limits. You can choose to have professionals invest your savings by putting the money into mutual funds specializing in fixed-income investments such as bonds, money-market securities or mortgages. You can switch your money from one type of fund to another.

These choices give you some control over how your money is invested, but it is limited. This may be a good thing if you do not take the time and trouble to learn the basics of do-it-yourself investing. If you do want to do it yourself, you can choose a self-directed RRSP. Within the limits of the tax rules, you can use these plans to invest in whatever you want. You decide whether to opt for the safety of guaranteed investments such as term deposits, seek out capital gains while risking capital losses in bonds, or blow the whole bundle on poorly chosen company stocks. The responsibility is yours and it should not be taken lightly. A professional investment adviser may be needed. Investing with before-tax dollars means that the government does share in your losses but it doesn't cover all of them. You lose, too.

Strip bonds are an ideal fixed-income investment for self-directed RRSPs. These are essentially promises to pay an amount of money at a future date, which you buy at a price discounted sufficiently to provide you at maturity with the results of today's available compounded rates of interest (see Chapter 12). You can choose maturities to coincide more or less with your retirement. The problem is that the tax rules normally oblige you to include in your taxable income each year the annual amount of interest earned but not actually paid to you. Put a strip bond in your RRSP, however, and you defer that obligation until you cash in the plan.

Choosing a self-directed RRSP also involves understanding the limits on investments imposed by the tax rules. Breaking those limits can bring you costly financial penalties. Most notably, you can put only a portion of an RRSP portfolio into foreign investments. The limit is 20 per cent of the original cost or book value of the investments in the plan. This effectively means that 80 per cent of each tax-deductible dollar must be invested in Canada. The penalty is a tax of 1 per cent a month on the excess. Canadian tax breaks are used mostly to encourage investment in Canada, even if that is the worst idea in the world for an investor at the time.

You can, however, protect yourself somewhat against a collapse in the Canadian dollar by buying Canadian government or corporate bonds that were sold for foreign currency in the first place, often for U.S. dollars. The interest on these is paid in the foreign currency and so is the eventual repayment of principal. If the value of the foreign currency rises during the life of the bonds, you will make a profit on the foreign exchange when you switch the interest and principal back into Canadian currency. Of course, if it falls, you will lose out. These do not have to be counted as foreign investments.

Similar rules govern investments under your RRIF. These devices offer an alternative to life annuities for reducing the taxman's bite on savings accumulated in an RRSP. To obtain an annual annuity payment for the rest of your life, however long or short, you hand over some or all of your savings to a life insurance company. The money is invested by the company. With a RRIF, you retain ownership and investment control of your savings. You have to withdraw and pay tax on a minimum annual amount from your RRIF, but you can withdraw more. The formula is designed to produce increasing minimum payments each year, rising to a 20 per cent maximum. These rules allow you to keep a RRIF going for your lifetime and your spouse's, too, if the capital lasts that long. Typically, a RRIF provides smaller amounts of income than an annuity in the early years but larger amounts in the later years. If you live long and invest unwisely, though, you may run out of money. As with most investment arrangements, more flexibility brings more responsibility.

CHAPTER 19

You Must Keep Score

MANY PEOPLE DABBLE IN investing like they dabble in other things. They find themselves with some unspent money and stick it into the first term deposit they come across, acting without rhyme or reason. They decide they really should start saving for retirement and they open the first registered retirement savings plan they hear about. Then they make things worse by tossing the confirmation notices and statements they receive into a drawer. At tax return time, they scramble to make sense of their investments and account for their investment profits, if any, to the tax collectors.

In the next chapter, you will find a discussion of the dangers of winging it with your precious savings, and of how to set about planning a portfolio of fixed-income investments suitable for your age, income and temperament. First, however, you need to know where you are before you can make an informed decision about where you should be going. As the road sweeper observed to the hapless motorist, you probably can't get there from here — at least not without a map showing where you've been. Your investment map consists of the proper records you should start keeping the moment you make the decision to rent your money out in a systematic way.

These records serve three vital purposes. They help keep the tax collectors happy and out of your life. They help you stay on top of your investments in an organized way, which becomes increasingly important once you build a sizable portfolio. They also enable you to keep score of how you are doing. Are you making a profit from your investments, both before and after inflation and before and after taxes? If you are not, you can perhaps change your strategy and tactics. In contrast, if you don't know whether you are making a profit, you won't know whether you should change anything. Investing without keeping proper records is like flying an airplane without working instruments.

The starting point for all your records is the piece of paper you get when you make an investment. Sometimes you may get several pieces of paper. At the bank counter you will get a passbook in which your savings deposits and withdrawals will be recorded, plus interest earned and less any service charges. Keep your passbooks up to date and keep track of the interest and charges. You may find you are lending fairly large amounts of money to the bank without getting any rent on it. Perhaps it's even costing you money to lend your money to the bank through your savings account. If so, that is a cue to reconsider the way you handle your temporary savings and perhaps to change the type of account you use.

When you buy a term deposit or investment certificate, you may get a record of the transaction at the time. In any case, you should make a personal note of the key information right away, before you forget it. This should include at least the amount, the maturity date, the promised interest rate and when it is paid. When the written confirmation of your deal arrives, check to make sure that what you got was what you thought you were buying. With the best of intentions, mistakes can be made, especially in verbal transactions. As movie magnate Sam Goldwyn observed once, "A verbal contract isn't worth the paper it's written on." If you don't understand something, check with the financial company right away. If there has been a mistake, get it corrected right away.

If you buy savings bonds, you should get a receipt giving similar information right away. Check to make sure your order is recorded exactly as you gave it. Later you should receive the actual savings bond certificates in the denominations you asked for. Again check that you have got what you ordered, then put the bonds in a safe place such as a safety deposit box. They are valuable documents and losing them will at the very least cause you considerable inconvenience. You can get replacements from the Bank of Canada, but that will be more difficult without proper records.

Purchases of bonds, money-market securities, mortgage-backed securities and mutual fund securities will also be confirmed in writing by the organization through which you buy them. In some cases, if you want them, you will get certificates in due course. These are also valuable documents and should be treated like cash and locked away in a safe place. In addition to the amount, maturity and interest rate, you need to have a record of your purchase price and the yield the security offers on your investment. Purchases and sales for

A Sample Fixed-Income Portfolio Report

Holdings	Security	Current price	Market value	% of total value	Indic. interest or dividend rate	Indic. annual income	% Yield
Cash & equivalents							
$5,000	CSBs	$100.00	$5,000	12.4	7.50%	$375	7.5
$10,000	Can.T-Bills	$98.50	$9,850	24.4		$601	6.1
Total cash equivalents			$14,850	36.8		$976	6.6
Marketable bonds							
$10,000	Can.'02s	$104.60	$10,460	25.9	8.50%	$850	7.83*
$5,000	Hyd.Que.'98s	$103.60	$5,180	12.8	8.75%	$438	7.99*
Total marketable bonds			$15,640	38.7		$1,288	
Mortgage-backed securities							
$5,000	ABC '05s	$100.00	$5,000	12.4	8.50%	$425	8.5
Total mtge-backed securities			$5,000	12.4		$425	
Preferred shares							
200	XYZ Series 1	$24.50	$4,900	12.1	$1.50	$300	6.1
Total preferreds			$4,900	12.1		$300	6.1
TOTAL PORTFOLIO			$40,390	100.0		$2,989	7.4

*yield to maturity

TABLE XX

your registered retirement savings plans or registered retirement income funds should also be confirmed in writing.

If you are dealing with a broker, you should get monthly or at least quarterly reports showing where things stand. This report should include a record of any transactions during the month, the amount of any cash balance in the account plus interest credited, and your holdings of securities if they have been left with the brokerage firm for safekeeping. Check these statements closely. There can sometimes be discrepancies between them and the written confirmations of your transactions. If there is, get it sorted out right away. It gets harder to correct matters as time goes by.

These receipts, confirmations and monthly statements are the principal source material for your personal portfolio records. These records can be elaborate or quite simple, as long as they contain the minimum essential information. A portfolio report for your fixed-income investments should include at least the following columns:

Holdings: List the actual amount of cash and the face value of investments such as treasury bills and bonds.

Security: Give the name of the particular investment. List them in separate sections for cash and cash equivalents, bills, bonds, mortgage-backed securities, and whatever else you have.

Current price: Update this as often as you want.

Market value: For deposits, this is the same as you paid, unless you bought in at a discount. For bills and bonds, this is the current price multiplied by how many you have. Remember that bonds are in units of $1,000 face value but the price is quoted in units one-tenth the size. Thus, a bond quoted at 98 is actually valued at $980.

Percentage of total value: Calculate the market value of each deposit or security as a percentage of the total market value of the portfolio. Both the numerator and denominator in this calculation change as market prices change.

Interest rate: Record this from the original confirmation.

Annual income: Total the interest expected from all your holdings.

Yield: This is the percentage return on each dollar of your investment. For deposits bought at full price, it's the same as the interest rate. For bills and bonds, you should have found this out when you bought them, and then you update it as market prices change.

This short list of column headings has some practical advantages. It may be possible to get all the information on one sheet of paper. In addition, it should concentrate your attention on the most important things you should know about your portfolio. Note that you should always see your total investment as the current market value of your portfolio, not just the original cost. Deciding to hold on to your investments is just as much an investment decision as the original purchases. You could cash many of them in at the current market price and spend the money. It's their current market value you are renting out now, not the amount you invested in the first place.

You can, and probably should, expand your records with a column showing the purchase price or initial investment, another showing the dollar gain or loss on holdings whose market value changes, and perhaps others showing the simple percentage gain or loss and the annual rate of gain or loss. You could get fancier still and compare these figures with an index of total returns on bonds and money-market securities. Financial publications carry these indexes or your broker should have access to one. You should, at least, always be aware of the current rate of inflation so that you know whether you are ahead of the game after taxes.

You will need to keep a record of any commissions you paid. These are added to your original cost and deducted from the sale proceeds when you calculate your capital gains and losses. They reduce the amount of any gain and increase the amount of any loss.

You can enter all this information manually in a book or on ledger sheets, making sure you keep all the original records of purchases and sales in case a suspicious tax auditor comes calling. But you will have to update those records whenever you do something with your fixed-income investments or as the market prices of tradable securities change. You can do this manually, too, especially if the list of your investments is short. You check the reports of prices and yields of fixed-income securities published in newspapers and specialist financial publications or in your broker's statements, update your figures and recalculate things as necessary.

Entering any new numbers and recalculating the various percentages can become a drag, however, especially for a large portfolio. This is where a personal computer can come in handy. No one should acquire such a machine merely to keep track of their personal finances, unless they invest on a huge scale in a large number of different sorts of securities. There's no denying, though, how much easier a computer makes the job. The machine will remember perfectly everything you tell it. Then it will calculate within seconds everything needed to keep proper score, with total accuracy. It will also report back to you everything you want to know about the investments you have already bought.

Any number of personal financial software packages are available from U.S. suppliers at moderate cost. Their principal job is to keep all your personal and household accounts. Some also enable you to keep the books of a small business. These packages will certainly do the job of record-keeping and analysis of your investment portfolio. Some come with the ability to link your computer by modem to electronic services that will feed you market prices, trading volumes and other investment information over your telephone line. In some cases, you can even get a chart of the information drawn on the screen in front of you, which is great fun. Gathering information this way is expensive, however, and will deplete your investment profits quickly if you are not careful. It's really only worth it for big-time players, for people whose employers pay the bills and for those who find it a reasonable price to pay for an absorbing hobby. It's cheaper than vintage motor cars or golf.

There are some drawbacks to the U.S. packages. They provide for things that have no counterpart in Canada, and may not provide for things that Canada has. The U.S. has individual retirement accounts, or IRAs. Canada has RRSPs. They are sort of the same thing, but not quite. At the least, the different terminology is irritating.

More serious is the fact that the tax-record and analysis services provided by the U.S. packages are useless to Canadians, because of the major differences in the income tax systems of the two countries. As well as the fundamental national differences, Canadian tax rules vary somewhat between provinces. In particular, a tax-preparation package prepared for residents of other provinces will be of no use to a Quebecker unless it has been adapted to that province's separate set of rules. Quebeckers get to do two quite different returns each year: one for Ottawa and one for Quebec City, and their federal return is itself different from the single federal and provincial tax returns used in other provinces. This added complexity may be one reason why good general-purpose Canadian personal financial software packages have been slower to appear, although there are packages that do parts of the job.

What no computer will do is decide what you should invest in, and whether to cash in any or all of your investments. There is software designed to provide reliable guidance on picking stocks, according to the claims of its authors. Whatever you may think of such claims, fixed-income investment decisions mostly involve making an informed judgment on the future trend of interest rates. This is a task for which common sense is more useful than electronic logic. It is, therefore, still reserved for human minds, which is kind of reassuring.

CHAPTER 20

Plan, Don't Wing It

SHOULD A 55-YEAR-OLD FATHER with few assets risk his small amount of savings on a penny mining stock on the Vancouver Stock Exchange? Clearly not. That is too obviously a case of the wrong investment at the wrong time for the wrong investor. But what about the more sensible younger investor who buys some high-yield strip bonds for the long haul but then neglects to put them into a tax-sheltered registered retirement savings plan? Each year he is faced with paying tax on income he has not received, and won't receive until the strip bonds pay off in full many years down the road. What about a careless investor who buys a $100,000 investment certificate from the one trust company that happens to go broke this year? Sure, he will get back $60,000 from the government deposit insurance system, but there's a good chance he will lose the remaining $40,000. These are not smart moves, either.

Running a personal portfolio of fixed-income investments is too important to be done on a hit-and-miss basis. Your savings dollars are difficult to come by in the first place. Renting them out in the various ways described in this book will make you more money. It's not something you should do on a whim, however. True, fixed-income investors are less likely to be caught up in the kind of crazes that grip stock-market investors. It's rare to have somebody breathlessly pass on a hot tip on the latest wrinkle in term deposits, or to promise you that your Canada bond will double in 12 months. But you must still keep your wits about you, even if you never go near the stock market.

One problem with fixed-income investing is that it's easy to be lulled into thinking there are no risks. By and large, there is a much smaller risk of losing your original capital when you rent your money out to earn interest than when you go in search of capital gains in the stock market. True, government deposit insurance covers your risk only within limits and not at all if you buy bonds and other marketable securities. But by spreading your money only among insured and top-quality borrowers, the odds are good that you will always get back every dollar you invested in the first place, plus the promised interest.

Even so, like every other sort of investor, you still face the three wicked witches of money management: inflation, taxes and interest-rate swings.

Inflation is measured by the annual rise in a representative collection of consumer prices. It's best thought of, though, as the annual decline in what each dollar can buy. Today, we tend to think of an annual inflation rate of about 3.2 per cent — the average for the last 10 years — as not too bad, as something we can live with. Maybe so, but its impact must never be forgotten by investors, who must also keep in mind that the much lower recent inflation rate is considered abnormal.

Suppose you drop a dollar coin into a corner of a drawer today and forget about it for the next 18 years. Then you unexpectedly find it and take it out to the store to see what it will buy. Assume also that inflation averaged 4 per cent annually during the years the dollar coin was missing from your life. How much will the loonie be worth in terms of purchasing power then? Recall the Rule of 72 from the first chapter. Divide four into 72 and what do you get? Eighteen, right? So in 18 years your loonie will really be worth just 50 cents. Even more dismaying, if inflation averages 10 per cent, your loonie will be worth less than a quarter in 18 years. It will halve in value in just over seven years.

This is why idle money is expensive money. If you do nothing else with it, you must put it where it will earn some interest, preferably more than the rate of inflation. These days, that is fairly easy. For historical reasons, today's interest rates well exceed the inflation rate (see Chapter 21). This has not always been so, and it may not always be so in the future. Right now, though, it makes renting out your money a more attractive proposition.

Staying ahead of inflation is no good, however, if you don't stay ahead after income taxes. In the top tax brackets in Canada, you can find yourself handing over more than 50 cents or so of every dollar of interest to help keep governments in the style to which they have become accustomed. This can play havoc with fixed-income investors. You invest $1,000 in a five-year investment certificate at, say, 7 per cent. Inflation averages 3.5 per cent over the five years, so you are ahead by 3.5 per cent a year, compounded if you reinvest the interest at the same rate.

That's nice, you think, until you remember taxes. If 50 cents of each dollar of interest goes to the tax collectors each year, your real after-tax return is just 3.5 per cent a year. So what's your real return after inflation is taken into account as well? A big fat nothing. Sure, you get every dollar you were promised. Sure, it's a better deal than losing ground from leaving the $1,000 idle. Emerging where you started doesn't get you very far, though.

Then there are interest-rate swings. Sure, they present opportunities. But they also pose problems. Suppose that your $1,000 is locked away for five years in that 7 per cent investment certificate while interest rates are dropping to the point where the going rate on such certificates eventually averages 10 per cent annually. You would be justifiably pleased with yourself. What seemed a good idea at the time really was a good idea. It can happen the other way around, though. Interest rates might soar and the going rate paid on such certificates might eventually average 15 per cent annually over the five years your money is locked away. You would be kicking yourself for not buying one-year certificates, wouldn't you?

Of the three major risks, there is not a lot you can do as a fixed-income investor about the toll of inflation — except to press the government to keep it under control and hope to invest your savings at a time when there is at least a small reward after inflation for lending your money instead of spending it. Doing more than that involves using some of your savings to seek the higher average returns offered by the stock market.

This underlines the importance of having an overall investment plan. As well as deciding how to diversify your fixed-income investments according to age, wealth and temperament, you have to decide how much of your total savings, if any, should go into other forms of investment such as the stock market. There have been quite long periods, most notably the 1970s, when the return from renting your money out did not even keep you level with inflation before taxes. After taxes, you were losing a bundle. Largely because of the memory of this, during most of the 1980s investors refused to accept anything less than a substantial real return after inflation from renting their money. With their interest and capital gains sheltered from taxes in, say, registered retirement savings plans, fixed-income investors did very well from 1983 through 1990. Inflation dropped sharply, then stabilized in the 4 to 5 per cent range, while interest rates stayed quite high.

By early 1991, however, this started to change. Interest rates fell sharply because of an economic recession, dramatically cutting the rent available on your savings. Inflation hardly budged at first. So after inflation and taxes, money-renters no longer did so well. Meanwhile, the stock market soared as investors began to anticipate the end of the recession and renewed economic growth that would improve company profits. By early 1992, inflation was falling faster than interest rates, and this phenomenon continued through 1993 to 1995. Actual dollars of interest shrank, but the real after-inflation return on a fixed-income investment increased.

This ebb and flow of returns on different sorts of investments is a continuing phenomenon. On average and over the long run, putting some of your savings into the stock market will increase your wealth more quickly than if you always stayed out of stocks, as long as you pay attention to what you are doing. There has to be a long enough time, however, for the odds to work in your favour. This suggests that, other things being equal, you can take more risks with your money when you are younger because you have more time to recover from temporary setbacks. Conversely, it probably does not make a lot of sense to put all or most of your accumulated savings into the stock market on the eve of your retirement, even if you are convinced that the greatest bull market in history is just getting under way. There's a chance you could be wrong and your savings could shrink, instead of expanding, at exactly the wrong time in your life.

Other things are never equal, of course. Putting all your savings in the stock market at age 25 certainly gives you a good chance of seeing the long-term odds work for you. Typically, though, people in their late 20s have more pressing uses for whatever is left over after meeting daily living expenses. Setting aside an emergency fund is a high priority, for instance, and that money should never go into the stock market. To earn some return on it, your emergency fund should be parked in the safest forms of fixed-income investment that also allow you to get at the money immediately if you need it. In practice, this means either government savings bonds or personal savings accounts. For couples in their 20s and early 30s, buying a house is also probably a better use for available savings than venturing into the stock market.

In the investment industry's life-cycle approach to solving financial conundrums, there are seven adult stages of life. First come the early earning years up to, say, 35. A potential investor is typically preoccupied by starting a career, setting up a family and establishing a home. The top priorities are some near-cash investments for emergencies and a savings plan. If money is available for investing after providing for these more urgent priorities, it could well go into the stock market and be directed into companies that show good prospects of capital gains rather than high dividend income.

Next come the middle earning years, from around 35 to 55 or so. Typically, living expenses decline in relation to income in this period and savings should increase. With more discretionary income available, as well as the need to minimize taxes, the stock market is again a good spot for part of a personal investment portfolio. The proportion could vary between a third and a half — depending on temperament, willingness to put some time and effort into the difficult art of stock market investing and the general investment environment.

In the late 50s, as retirement looms, the safety of your investments becomes more important. Because of inflation and taxes, it is still worthwhile for people with substantial savings and high incomes to diversify their portfolios with stock market investments as well as fixed-income investments. Advantage should be taken of bull markets to sell higher-risk stocks and concentrate on the stocks of good-quality, well-established companies that pay regular dividends as well as increase in market price. The average life of fixed-income investments should also be gradually reduced to lessen the risk of having to cash them in after retirement at a bad time.

Finally, in the years of retirement, investors typically have to cope with a fixed income and the need to make sure that their savings outlive them. Except for people wealthy enough not to worry about such things, the stock market is of limited interest. Renting your money out in safe fixed-income investments at the highest possible return is the top priority, preferably in ways that lessen or eliminate the tax bite. Because of the favourable treatment given by the tax collector to dividends, some dividend-paying stocks of high-quality, blue-chip companies may be worth considering, but only with caution. Counting on high-growth stocks to protect you against the ravages of inflation is not a good idea in your retirement years because such stocks are by definition riskier and you may not have enough time for the odds on better returns in the stock market to pay off.

You can, however, do something major about the tax risk. Recall that interest income bears tax at your top rate (see Chapter 18). From this emerges the golden rule of fixed-income investing: Try to put all interest-earning investments, beyond emergency savings, into the two best tax shelters available to individuals — a registered retirement savings plan or a registered retirement income fund. Your interest income will accumulate and compound gratifyingly without the taxman taking a costly bite of it each year. True, you may become liable for tax on your profits eventually, but you can defer that for a very long time.

There are two ways to deal with the dangers of interest-rate swings. One is the aggressive approach. You credit yourself with the ability to outguess the financial markets and to predict the timing and direction of changes in interest accurately. Then you go out and try to prove it with your savings. If you think interest rates are heading downward for a while, you commit all your money for a long period of, say, five years at today's rates. You buy bonds at discounted prices and plan to sell them at premium prices when your prediction comes true, preferably just before interest rates start heading skyward again. Maybe you even add some icing to the cake and back your prediction with some bond options. Of course, if you think interest rates are going nowhere but up from here, you rent your money out only for very short periods of time, reasoning that you will be able to get a higher rent for it very soon. You happily sell any bonds you own to people who misguidedly believe the opposite to you, and you wait for the opportunity to buy them back more cheaply later on.

This sort of thing can be great fun and highly rewarding if you get it right. Perhaps you are even one of a small minority of people who claim to be able to play interest-rate swings profitably most of the time. If you really can, you don't need my help. You don't have to take the second, more cautious, approach recommended for the rest of us. This is based on diversification. You spread your savings around different types of borrowers and you vary the length of the lease on your money, too.

It works this way. A portion of your fixed-income portfolio always goes into something you can get at in a hurry if you need it and which always repays you 100 cents on the dollar at any time. This desirable quality is known as 100 per cent liquidity. Government savings bonds are an ideal example. So is cash, except the interest is lousy.

Another portion goes into interest-earning cash equivalents such as three-month treasury bills or a money-market fund. These don't provide 100 per cent liquidity but they come pretty close. You may lose a little bit if you have to cash in when interest rates have moved up. It won't be much, though, and the interest returns on your money are better.

Then, depending on your age, wealth and temperament, you can put a remaining portion into either longer-term deposits and investment certificates, or into securities whose prices swing along with interest rates but in the opposite direction. Your temperament should be the principal deciding factor. If you are the kind who can't sleep for worrying about what your bonds are doing, best stick to deposits and certificates. One source of worry will be removed from your life. You will still probably regret taking a five-year deal after watching interest rates rise since you handed over the money, but at least you won't be watching the market price fall as well. At such times, it can be hard to remember that if you hold on until your bonds mature, the odds are that you will get all your money back and earn exactly the amount of interest you were promised.

Assuming your nerves can stand it, you should then consider your age and your wealth. One of the major advantages of youth is that you have time to recover from your mistakes. Loading up on bonds in the early stages of a major down market, like the second half of the 1970s, is a big mistake. If you did it on the eve of retirement and needed to sell them at much lower prices than you paid, it could be a catastrophe. But if you did it at the age of 35, it would probably be merely a costly lesson. The odds are you could have hung on until the bonds paid off at maturity, and you might even have sold some at a premium during the bull market for bonds in the early 1980s.

The moral is that the older you get, the more important liquidity becomes. It's like insurance: You have to pay for the protection by passing up some opportunities for profit, but it will be worth it if you ever have to collect. With insurance, it's the risk of your house burning down. With investments, it's the danger of facing a cash crisis and having to sell your marketable securities at unexpectedly low prices.

This is why your wealth is also a factor. Cash crises are more likely in the lives of people of moderate means. Liquidity in your investments becomes less important as your assets multiply and your liabilities diminish, although even some very wealthy people have been caught in a vicious liquidity squeeze from time to time. Being asset-rich but cash-poor is not unknown among the sort of people most of us would consider very well off. Come to think of it, that is a comforting, if uncharitable, reflection.

CHAPTER 21

Assessing the Future

RENTING OUT YOUR MONEY was a rewarding business throughout the 1980s. In most years, the total return exceeded the rate of inflation by a handy margin, meaning you gained ground in real terms. That's counting both the interest you received and the capital gains you might have made if you reinvested everything at prevailing interest rates and prices. Taxes would have sliced away much of this profit, but from this book you have learned several ways to shelter your gains from the tax collector — at least for a while.

Is this likely to be the experience of money-renters in the 1990s? Not likely. This decade probably won't be quite as rewarding. And there is a division of opinion when it comes to the future direction of fixed-income investing.

One of the two schools of thought believes that lending money to top-quality borrowers — that is, those that are the most likely to pay it back — will be the safest game in town. If these pessimists are right in their prediction of a long period of economic decline, doing anything riskier with your money than lending it to the government will be very perilous, and even that degree of caution may not save you from financial disaster.

The second school of thought holds that the 1980s were an aberration in the normal relationship between average rates of return on the major classes of investment. If this is the case, the final decade of the 20th century will see the return of stocks to their proper place in the profitability ranking: first. Long-term government bonds will be in their proper second place, and short-term money-market securities such as treasury bills will be back in third place. This ranking reflects what seems the natural order of things — the greater the risk, the greater the reward. If, on average and over time, investors in stocks did not make more on their money than from renting it out by buying bonds and bills, they would eventually stop buying stocks entirely.

Interestingly, over the very long term that relationship has persisted despite the aberration of the last decade. Take a look at Table XXI. It shows total returns for varying periods in Canada for the three principal categories of investment. The figures, calculated by the Canadian actuarial and pension consultant Towers Perrin, take into account capital gains and losses as well as income from dividends and interest. Note that over the more than 60 years from 1926 through 1995 the average annual return on representative Canadian stocks was almost 10 per cent. Over the same period the average annual return on government treasury bills was 4.8 per cent. On long-term government bonds it was 5.9 per cent. Remember that those years included a major economic boom in the 1920s, a terrible economic slump in the 1930s, a World War and several other wars and political convulsions.

The relationship between returns on the different classes of investment is even more striking when the decline in the purchasing power of each dollar of investment profit is taken into account. The compound annual inflation rate averaged 3.3 per cent over the same 68 years. When that is subtracted from the results, treasury bills weigh in with an annual average of 1.5 per cent real return. The bonds show an annual average of 2.6 per cent. For stocks, the average real return is a much more impressive 6.6 per cent.

Note, however, how the gap narrows when figures for the last 25 years are calculated. More striking still, 10-year figures show bonds at the head of the list.

So what happened in the 1980s? There is a clue in the inflation rate figures in the Towers Perrin table. Notice how inflation averaged 6 per cent over the last 25 years but slowed to an average 3.2 per cent in the last decade. The first figure reflects the great upsurge in inflation during the late 1960s and the 1970s. The second reflects the dramatic slowdown in inflation during the 1980s and early 1990s.

Around 1980 and 1981, the buyers of bonds seemed finally to realize they had been had. Year after year during the previous decade they had rented their money to governments and companies on terms that gave them little or no return after inflation and taxes. The annual drop in the purchasing power of the dollars with which they were paid was frequently larger than the amount of interest they

Key Facts of Investment Returns

COMPOUND ANNUAL RETURN INCLUDING INCOME

	1926-1995	Last 25 years	Last 10 years
Treasury bills	4.8%	9.3%	8.8%
Government bonds (long-term)	5.9	9.9	11.9
Stocks (TSE 300)	9.9	10.7	8.3
Inflation rate (compounded annually)	3.3	6.0	3.2

SOURCE: TOWERS PERRIN

TABLE XXI

were getting. It's hard to believe, but in 1981 the compound annual return on long-term Canadian government bonds after inflation was — 12.5 per cent, according to Towers Perrin calculations. This was not a flash in the pan. Over the five years through 1981 the annual average was — 15 per cent. Over the 10 years through 1981 it was — 5.74 per cent.

Yet the very next year, in 1982, the real return on such bonds soared to a startling 31.67 per cent. Clearly, something extraordinary happened between 1981 and 1982. What happened first was a revolt of bond buyers, who refused any longer to lose their savings to inflation. They demanded and got super-high interest rates to lend any money at all, and then only for short periods. For a brief period in 1981 the Canadian government paid more than 20 per cent interest on its three-month treasury bills. Rates required to sell short-term government bonds soared close to 20 per cent and new long-term government bonds could not be sold at any price. Most companies could not sell regular-style bonds, either.

The revolt finally pushed governments in Canada and the U.S. into an all-out crackdown on inflation and a sharp economic recession followed. Inflation dropped sharply, which was no surprise. Less expected was the phenomenon of inflation staying down even when a new economic boom got under way in 1983. The hard-won credibility established by the governments and their central bankers seemed to have vaccinated the economy against a recurrence of inflationary fever. The rate remained in a historically high but stable range of 4 to 5 per cent for most of the decade.

Because this was not expected, interest rates came down much more slowly. Investors who remembered their inflation-caused losses during the 1970s were cautious and took care always to demand a good margin of safety in interest rates. They behaved on the assumption that the slowdown in inflation was only temporary and that they would not allow themselves to be mugged by it again. Oddly, their predecessors in the 1970s were working on a similar assumption — that the upsurge in inflation was temporary. The memory of all the years of low inflation in the 1930s, 1940s and 1950s held sway long after it was no longer relevant to current conditions.

As a result, throughout most of the decade the real returns enjoyed by investors from renting their money out were unusually high, even after allowing for the still continuous decline in the purchasing power of each dollar of interest and repayments of capital. This was what skewed the normal relationship between returns on different categories of investment in that decade. By 1987, however, with a long-running bull market in stocks supplanting bonds as the centre of attention for investors, there were signs that a more normal relationship was returning. This continued in 1988 and 1989, but the collapse of the stock market in 1990 interrupted it again. By early 1991, however, stocks were back in the limelight as share prices rallied strongly and the real rates of return on interest-bearing investments were crimped between falling interest rates and more or less stable inflation. In early 1992, real rates of return climbed once more as inflation collapsed. But in 1993 a strong bull market in stocks helped reinforce the belief that they are resuming their traditional top-dog position.

Another lesson for investors emerges from study of the figures on returns from different categories of investment. Stocks do offer the highest average return over the long run, but the return varies greatly from year to year. This shows why many investors should invest in vehicles other than shares. Stocks are inherently a riskier investment than renting your money out. You need both time and good judgment for the odds to work in your favour. The time needed can be lessened by paying attention and working hard at choosing your own stock market investments. Those with not enough time can also reap the stock market's bigger rewards by casting a wide net in the form of well-chosen mutual funds specializing in stocks.

Many people can do neither, however. They do not have the time or the temperament to handle do-it-yourself stock market investing, nor sufficient savings with which to spread risks. But everybody can rent their money out profitably — beginning perhaps with savings deposits, guaranteed investment certificates and savings bonds, then graduating to the various more complicated forms of interest-earning investments described in this book.

Renting your money can be as simple or as complicated as you like. It can take just a few minutes of your time every now and then, or can become an absorbing and rewarding hobby. Remember that most hobbies cost you money instead of making it.

Early in 1994, the central bankers began raising rates once more, to slow economic growth that was considered too fast to last, and so head off a revival in inflation. Those rate hikes kicked the props from under the bond and stock markets during 1994, despite a powerful recovery in corporate profits. But by early 1995 it had become clear they had done their job as the economy paused for breath. So once again interest rates fell and bond and stock prices rose.

At mid-1996, the big unanswered question was whether the central bankers had overdone it again and allowed the economy to accelerate in an unsustainable spurt, or had they successfully engineered a so-called soft landing — that is, slower but sustainable economic growth with low inflation, a sort of economic nirvana.

Meanwhile, as governments across Canada reduced or eliminated their deficits, the prospect appeared that existing government bonds will develop a scarcity value. Successive up and down cycles in the economy, matched by up and down cycles in interest rates, seem eternal features of the landscape of the industrial world. They provide alert investors with many opportunities to increase the return from renting their money.

Good luck in your money-renting career.

A Glossary of Terms

ADJUSTED COST BASE is what the taxman figures an investment cost you for the purpose of calculating your capital gains or losses. This amount includes commissions, which are easy to calculate, and other items that are not – thanks to today's ridiculously complicated tax rules.

BEARS are investors who believe interest rates are more likely to go up than down in the next little while. If they are right, the prices of existing fixed-income securities such as bonds will go down.

BONDS are IOUs issued by governments and companies in exchange for money they borrow. They are promises to repay the borrowed money at some fixed future date, which may be in one year or 30 years, and in the meantime to pay interest usually at some stated interest rate. Once issued to the original investors, they can be bought and sold in the bond market.

BULLS are investors who believe interest rates are more likely to go down than up in the next little while. If they are right, the prices of existing fixed-income securities such as bonds will go up.

CALL OPTION is a contract that gives you the right to buy a bond or any other available investment at a fixed price before a certain date. You buy one if you are convinced the investment's market price will go up soon and you want to magnify your profit by using leverage (see below). If you are wrong, the option will expire worthless, which most do.

CONVERTIBLES are bonds or preferred shares that can be exchanged by their owners usually for common shares of the company that issued them. They offer a two-way bet by providing some interest to begin with, plus the possibility of profiting handsomely if the company does well. Their appeal is often more theoretical than real, however.

CURRENT YIELD is how much you get in interest as a percentage of the amount you have invested. A $100 savings bond paying $10 interest a year provides a current yield of 10 per cent. The current yield of investments whose market price changes varies inversely with the price. If the price of a $1,000 bond paying 10 per cent interest or $100 a year falls to $800, the current yield rises to 12.5 per cent (100 divided by 800, and the result multiplied by 100). That's not the full story, however (see YIELD TO MATURITY).

DEBENTURES are another form of bond. There are some technical legal differences but today the terms are used interchangeably.

LBOs, short for leveraged buyouts, are deals in which a company is bought with a lot of borrowed money frequently raised through selling high-yield and high-risk junk bonds. Often, the buyers are the company's own management. The idea is to handle the repayments out of the company's own cash, including what it can get for selling off some or even all of its assets. This was a popular activity in the 1980s and some of the early deals even made sense. By the end of the decade, though, the corporate landscape was littered with LBO disasters and many buyers of junk bonds realized that was exactly what they had invested in.

LEVERAGE in the financial world is making one dollar do the work of many. There are a host of variations but all have one thing in common: If you are right, your profits will be magnified, and so will your losses if you are wrong.

LIQUIDITY in the bond or money markets can be good or poor. If it's good, that means there are enough securities of a particular type and issue available for trading so they can be bought or sold in reasonable quantities with small price changes between transactions. If it's poor, that means there are not enough.

PONZI SCHEME is the classic financial scam in which early investors in a supposedly get-rich-quick venture are paid out of the money taken in from later investors. It lasts only as long as more and more investors can be induced to come in, expanding like a bubble. When it bursts, the effects are nasty. Named for Charles Ponzi, who took many unwary U.S. investors this way in 1919-20, there are many variations including the perennial chain letter. The fact that it still works justifies the con man's boast that there's a mug born every minute.

PREFERRED SHARES entitle their owner to a fixed dividend each year out of the company's profit. There is no guarantee the company will always pay the dividend, but at least you are in line ahead of the owners of the common shares because the company can't pay them without paying you first.

PUT OPTION is a contract that gives you the right to sell a security such as a bond at a fixed price before a certain date. You buy one if you believe interest rates are going up soon and therefore bond prices will go down and you want a small bet to pay off big by using leverage (see above). If you are wrong, the option will expire worthless, which most do.

UNDERWRITER in the bond market means a brokerage firm or group of firms that has promised to buy a new issue of bonds from a government or company at a fixed discounted price, subject to some weasel clauses, and to arrange the resale of the bonds to investors in general at the full price. The underwriting profit is the difference, if any, between the discounted price the underwriter pays and what it gets from the investors. There can also be an underwriting loss if things go badly.

WARRANTS sometimes come with a new issue of corporate bonds to make them more attractive. Normally, they are options to buy more shares in the company at a fixed price at any time before a certain date. Sometimes, you get the right to buy something else such as a bond or commodity such as gold. After the initial sale, they are usually detachable and are traded separately.

YIELD CURVE is the line plotted on a graph that shows the various yields to maturity of comparable short-, medium- and long-term fixed-income securities. It is described as normal, or positive, if the line slopes upward, flat if the yields are about the same and inverted, or negative, if yields are higher on short-term securities.

YIELD TO MATURITY is your investment return as a percentage of the amount you have invested in a bond whose price varies with market conditions. It takes into account both the interest you will receive during the life of the bond and the amount you will be paid when it matures. If you buy a $1,000 20-year bond that pays 10 per cent annual interest for a price of $1,000, the yield to maturity is the same as the current yield of 10 per cent. If you pay only $900 for it, however, the yield to maturity will be 11.7 per cent. It is higher than the current yield because as well as the promised interest payments, you can expect to receive $1,000 when the bond matures. The complicated calculation takes into account this capital gain and assumes the interest payments can be reinvested at the same rate. If you paid $1,200 for the bond, the future capital loss would make the yield to maturity less than the current yield. Used alone in discussions of the bond and money markets, yield usually means yield to maturity.

Bibliography

Most books on personal investing concentrate on the stock market, and many of them are of the get-rich-quick kind that you should avoid. There is a dearth of books specifically on fixed-income investing, a gap this book is designed to help fill.

For further study:

The Globe and Mail Personal Finance Library. Publisher: *The Globe and Mail.* A series of books, including this one, that provide basic as well as in-depth information on every facet of managing your money.

How to Invest in Canadian Securities. Publisher: Canadian Securities Institute. A shortened version of the correspondence course offered by the national educational organization for the investment industry. Updated regularly.

The Canadian Securities Course. Publisher: Canadian Securities Institute. The complete text of the correspondence course offered by the national educational organization of Canada's investment industry. The course is designed for trainee brokers but is available to the general public.

For further information and research:

Financial Post Corporation Service. Publisher: *The Financial Post.* A comprehensive reference source of factual information on Canadian companies with publicly traded shares. Also available on-line to your computer.

Info Globe. Publisher: *The Globe and Mail.* A comprehensive reference source of factual information on Canadian companies of use to investors equipped with computer and modem.

Infomart. Publisher: Southam. A similar computerized reference source of factual information on Canadian companies of use to investors equipped with computer and modem.

Index